What Must I Do to be Saved?
What Do the Scriptures Say?
A Catholic Perspective

By
Joseph C. Kindel

Published by
THE RIEHLE FOUNDATION
P.O. Box 7
Milford, OH 45150-0007

Nihil Obstat: Reverend Robert J. Buschmiller
                    August 19, 1995

Imprimatur: ✠ Most Reverend Carl K. Moeddel,
                    Vicar General and Auxiliary Bishop
                    Cincinnati, Ohio
                    August 28, 1995

Published by The Riehle Foundation

For additional copies, write:
                    The Riehle Foundation
                    P.O. Box 7
                    Milford, Ohio 45150-0007

All Scripture excerpts, except where noted, have been taken from the Revised Standard Version of the Bible, copyright 1946, 1952, 1971 by the Division of Christian Education of the National Council of the Churches of Christ in the U.S.A.

Remaining excerpts, marked NAB, are taken from The New American Bible, copyright 1970 by the Confraternity of Christian Doctrine, Washington, D.C.

Cover art by T. Veerkamp

ISBN: 1-877678-39-2

Library of Congress Catalog Card No.: 95-92598

Table of Contents

Introduction

This book was written to help build understanding between Catholics and other Christians. Many Catholics today have family members who are Christians of other denominations. This is often a cause of distress within the family. Can those family members who are not Catholic be saved, especially if they've rejected the faith they were baptized into? The other Christians, in turn, often having been converted to Bible-alone forms of Christianity, wonder if their Catholic relatives can be saved. This situation made me wonder, "What *does* the Bible teach about salvation?" Yes, there are a few often-quoted verses about faith and baptism, etc., but what does the *whole Bible* say about salvation?

This book is largely the result of a computer search which found all the verses in the Bible that contain such words and phrases as "salvation," "save," "saved," "kingdom," and "eternal life." These Scripture quotes were then expanded upon by combing through the new *Catechism of the Catholic Church* and several works on apologetics mentioned in the Suggested Reading list at the end of the book.

In this book you will find a selection of representative verses on the topic of salvation from the whole Bible, giving a wider perspective than is usual. The sections on Catholic teaching are taken mostly from the *Catechism of the Catholic Church*, where the reader is encouraged to go for more thorough teaching. The reader is also urged to go deeper into the Scriptures—to set aside this book and pick up the Bible whenever the Holy Spirit prompts. May the LORD Himself bring you to the fullness of joy as you prayerfully reflect on the good news of salvation.

Chapter 1

Why Do I Need to be Saved?

Why do I need to be saved? What from? The Scriptures speak of God saving us from many things: from our enemies, from evildoers, from affliction, pain, guilt and fear, from danger, trouble and oppression, from death. But the ultimate salvation is from eternal death, also called the second death or eternal damnation.

What is eternal damnation? Is this something to be feared? There are two major things we know about damnation: 1) it is total separation from God, Who alone is our happiness; 2) it is for ever and ever with no second chances. This is serious business.

In God alone lies our happiness. Without Him, we cannot find happiness in this life or the next:

> *Only in God be at rest, my soul, for from him comes my hope. He only is my rock and my salvation, my stronghold; I shall not be disturbed* (*Psalm* 62:6-7 NAB).

But our sins, if we continue in them, cut us off totally from the Source of our happiness, our fulfillment, our very life: *"Your iniquities have made a separation between you and your God"* (*Isaiah* 59:2). If we persist in our sins until the end of our life, we are in danger of hearing these words addressed to us by the Jesus, Just Judge of the Universe:

> *"Then he will say to those at his left hand, 'Depart from me, you cursed, into the eternal fire prepared for the devil and his angels' "* (*Matthew* 25:41).

Is it true that Hell isn't so bad—that its just a community of those who enjoy sinning? Jesus urges us to take the most extreme measures in this life to avoid damnation in the next:

> *"If your eye causes you to sin, pluck it out; it is better for you to enter the kingdom of God with one eye than with two eyes to be thrown into hell, where their worm does not die, and the fire is not quenched"* (*Mark* 9:47-48).

Some people believe that we will have another chance after this life, through reincarnation or some other means, but the Scriptures are clear: *"It is appointed for men to die once, and after that comes judgment"* (*Hebrews* 9:27). In the end, there is good news for those who love God and do what is right, but bad news for those who do evil:

> *"The Son of man will send his angels, and they will gather out of his kingdom all causes of sin and all evildoers, and throw them into the furnace of fire; there men will weep and gnash their teeth"* (*Matthew* 13:41-42).

What have I done that I would be in danger of suffering eternal damnation? St. Paul reminds us, *"All have sinned and fall short of the glory of God"* (*Romans* 3:23). "All" includes me. As Isaiah discovered in the awesome presence of God, *"I am a man of unclean lips, and I dwell in the midst of a people of unclean lips"* (*Isaiah* 6:5). As members of the human family, the personal destinies of each one of us are caught up in the destiny of the whole race. *"Sin came into the world through one man and death through sin, and so death spread to all men because all men sinned"* (*Romans* 5:12). Not only human beings but all of creation has suffered due to the sin of Adam: *"the creation waits with eager longing for the revealing of the sons of God . . . because the creation itself will be set free from its bondage to decay"* (*Romans* 8:19, 21).

Our sins have removed us from friendship with God since *"God is light and in him is no darkness at all"* (*1 John* 1:5).

*You were dead because of your sins and offenses. . . .
All of us were once of their company; we lived at the
level of the flesh, following every whim and fancy, and
so by nature deserved God's wrath like the rest
(Ephesians 2:1, 3 NAB).*

The creature has had the audacity to break from his Creator. *"Woe to him who contends with his Maker; a potsherd among potsherds of the earth"* (*Isaiah* 45:9 NAB).

Is there anything we can do to repair the damage caused by our sins? Is there any way we can persuade God to take us back to Himself? Is there any way we can appease Him? The answer to these questions is "No." There is no way we can win back God. *"Truly no man can ransom himself, or give to God the price of his life"* (*Psalm* 49:7). Is there any hope then? Can friendship between God and us be restored? Yes! *"For God has consigned all men to disobedience, that he may have mercy upon all"* (*Romans* 11:32). But His mercy must come to us through a Savior, since we are powerless to save ourselves.

Chapter 2

What Has God Done that I Might be Saved?

Fortunately for us, God has taken the initiative to win *us* back. He loves us and desires to restore us to His friendship. The LORD looks upon each of us and whispers, *"Ah, you are beautiful, my beloved, ah, you are beautiful"* (*Song of Songs* 1:15 NAB). Because of His great love for us, individually and as a people, God is willing to go to any length to win us back. Speaking to Israel (and to each one of us) as to an unfaithful wife who has utterly spurned her husband, God declares:

> *"In that day, says the LORD . . . I will betroth you to me for ever; I will betroth you to me in righteousness and in justice, in steadfast love, and in mercy. I will betroth you to me in faithfulness; and you shall know the LORD"* (*Hosea* 2:16, 19-20).

The story of God's plan to bring us back to Himself and our response to His invitation, the greatest love story of all time, is the story of the Bible. The Scriptures are full of verses like the following one:

> *The LORD is my light and my salvation; whom shall I fear?* (*Psalm* 27:1).

Over and over, the Bible reminds us that God Himself is our salvation; there is no other way to freedom. *"Turn to me and be safe, all you ends of the earth, for I am God; there is no other!"* (*Isaiah* 45:22 NAB).

And again, *" 'I, I am He who blots out your transgressions for my own sake, and I will not remember your sins' "* (*Isaiah* 43:25).

From the moment Adam and Eve broke God's command, even

5

before the consequences of their sin had fully taken effect, God began to declare His intention to win back mankind. Speaking to the serpent, God said, *"'I will put enmity between you and the woman, and between your seed and her seed; he shall bruise your head, and you shall bruise his heel'"* (*Genesis* 3:15). Over the centuries God announced more and more clearly His intention to save us. About six hundred years before Christ, He spoke the following words through the prophet Jeremiah:

> *"Behold, the days are coming, says the LORD, when I will make a new covenant with the house of Israel and the house of Judah. . . . I will put my law within them, and I will write it upon their hearts. . . . I will forgive their iniquity, and I will remember their sin no more"* (*Jeremiah* 31:31, 33, 34).

God did not bring about His promised salvation the way we would expect. In His wisdom, He began by choosing one nation from among all the nations on earth to work with, a people particularly His own. He chose them, not because they were a great nation, for they were the least of the nations, but because He loved them (see *Deuteronomy* 7:6-7). He bound Himself to them by covenant. The Israelites, God's chosen people, broke His covenant. Again and again, God reached out to His people, sending His messengers, the prophets. *"'They put to death those who foretold the coming of the Just One'"* (*Acts* 7:52 NAB). But God's plan could not be frustrated; despite the hardness of heart of His chosen people, God was preparing them to receive their Savior.

> *In times past, God spoke in fragmentary and varied ways to our fathers through the prophets; in this, the final age, he has spoken to us through his Son* (*Hebrews* 1:1-2 NAB).

But when the Father sent His only beloved Son into the world to save us, we rejected Him and nailed Him to a cross. Out of this crime, the most grievous in human history, God in the wonder of His creative love wrought our salvation.

Who is this Son, this Savior, sent to us by God?

He is the Word made flesh, the Son of God. He is also the son of Mary, the son of David, the son of Abraham, the son of Adam. He is the flower of the human race, the blossom of Israel. *"In days to come Jacob shall take root, Israel shall blossom and put forth shoots, and fill the whole world with fruit" (Isaiah* 27:6).

His name is "Jesus," which means "Yahweh is salvation." "Yahweh" is the divine name meaning "I AM WHO I AM" (see *Exodus* 3:14). So Jesus' name means "I AM WHO I AM am salvation." No wonder we say His is the *"name above every name" (Philippians* 2:9)!

Is Jesus truly divine, God Himself? Yes.

> *He is the image of the invisible God, the first-born of all creation; for in him all things were created, in heaven and on earth, visible and invisible. . . . all things were created through him and for him. He is before all things, and in him all things hold together. . . . For in him all the fullness of God was pleased to dwell. . . . In him the whole fullness of deity dwells bodily (Colossians* 1:15-16, 17, 19, 2:9).

St. John the Evangelist also makes Jesus' identity clear: *"In the beginning was the Word, and the Word was with God, and the Word was God" (John* 1:1).

Is Jesus truly human? Yes. He is the man-God.

> *Since therefore the children share in flesh and blood, he himself likewise partook of the same nature, that through death he might destroy him who has the power of death, that is, the devil, and deliver all those who through fear of death were subject to lifelong bondage. . . . Therefore he had to be made like his brethren in every respect. . . . For because he himself has suffered and been tempted, he is able to help those who are tempted (Hebrews* 2:14-15, 17-18).

Jesus, the promised Messiah, is the *only* way to the Father.

> *There is one God, and there is one mediator between
> God and men, the man Christ Jesus, who gave himself
> as a ransom for all (1 Timothy 2:5-6).*

Jesus said to Thomas, " '*I am the way, and the truth, and the
life; no one comes to the Father, but by me*' " (*John* 14:6). In
1 John 5:12 we read, "*He who has the Son has life; he who has
not the Son of God has not life.*"

Jesus said, " '*I am the door; if any one enters by me, he will be
saved and will go in and out and find pasture*' " (*John* 10:9).
Jesus also said,

> "*My sheep hear my voice, and I know them, and they
> follow me; and I give them eternal life, and they shall
> never perish, and no one shall snatch them out of my
> hand*" (*John* 10:27-28).

Was it necessary for Jesus to die so that we could be set free?
Are our sins that serious? Scripture says, "*Without the shedding
of blood there is no forgiveness of sins*" (*Hebrews* 9:22). Jesus,
by giving up His life-blood for His friends, has won for us a most
wonderful salvation:

> *He entered, not with the blood of goats and calves, but
> with his own blood, and achieved eternal redemption
> (Hebrews 9:12 NAB).*

> *Since, therefore, we are now justified by his blood,
> much more shall we be saved by him from the wrath of
> God. For if while we were enemies we were reconciled
> to God by the death of his Son, much more, now that
> we are reconciled, shall we be saved by his life
> (Romans 5:9-10).*

Not only has Jesus' death reconciled us with the Father, but
also with our brothers and sisters. St. Paul writes that reconciliation between Jew and Gentile, and therefore between every con-
ceivable enemy, has taken place in Jesus' flesh at the cost of His
shed blood:

> *But now in Christ Jesus you who once were far off*
> *have been brought near in the blood of Christ. For he*
> *is our peace, who has made us both one, and has bro-*
> *ken down the dividing wall of hostility . . . that he*
> *might create in himself one new man in place of the*
> *two, so making peace, and might reconcile us both to*
> *God in one body through the cross, thereby bringing*
> *the hostility to an end* (*Ephesians* 2:13-16).

Further, every other division brought about by our sins has been healed *"by means of him [who reconciled] everything in his own person, both on earth and in the heavens, making peace through the blood of his cross"* (*Colossians* 1:20 NAB). It was out of love for us that Jesus laid down His life for us to reconcile us with His Father. *"Greater love has no man than this, that a man lay down his life for his friends"* (*John* 15:13).

At the dawn of the nation of Israel, Abraham prophesied when he told his son Isaac, *" 'God will provide himself the lamb for a burnt offering' "* (*Genesis* 22:8). This prophecy was fulfilled some two thousand years later when *"the Word became flesh and made his dwelling among us"* (*John* 1:14 NAB). John the Baptist, sent by God to announce the Messiah, *"saw Jesus coming toward him, and said, 'Behold the Lamb of God, who takes away the sin of the world!' "* (*John* 1:29).

Although God began His plan of salvation by choosing a single people, in Jesus His salvation has been extended to us all. *"Salvation is from the Jews"* (*John* 4:22), but all nations and all generations have been included. God declared through the prophet Isaiah, speaking of the Messiah:

> *It is too little, he says, for you to be my servant, to*
> *raise up the tribes of Jacob, and restore the survivors*
> *of Israel; I will make you a light to the nations, that*
> *my salvation may reach to the ends of the earth*
> (*Isaiah* 49:6 NAB).

Not only did God intend to rescue the people of every nation, but *"my justice shall remain forever and my salvation, for all generations"* (*Isaiah* 51:8 NAB). From the beginning God desired *"all men to be saved and to come to the knowledge of the truth"* (*1 Timothy* 2:4).

St. Paul gives us additional light on God's plan to save all mankind. Beginning with His chosen one, Abraham, God raised up a people, the Israelites, from his descendants. In each generation, only a remnant stayed faithful to God, while most of them fell away from Him. *"By their transgression salvation has come to the Gentiles"* (*Romans* 11:11 NAB)! Even those Israelites who fell away are not completely lost, for *"if the dough offered as first fruits is holy, so is the whole lump; and if the root is holy, so are the branches"* (*Romans* 11:16). St. Paul, wanting to make his point clearly, says:

> I want you to understand this mystery, brethren: a hardening has come upon part of Israel, until the full number of the Gentiles come in, and so all Israel will be saved (*Romans* 11:25-26).

Have you ever noticed how God repeatedly uses what looks like a tragedy to bring about a greater good? *"We know that God makes all things work together for the good of those who love God and are called according to his decree"* (*Romans* 8:28 NAB). Our salvation follows this pattern: out of our greatest crime, the murder of the Son of God, God draws our greatest good. This is cause for rejoicing!

The salvation of God far exceeds our loftiest hopes. Not only does He save us from danger, especially of the eternal kind, but He also sets us free for the abundant life (see *John* 10:10), free to love as He loves. He heals and restores us, desiring that we have life to the full, going so far as to allow us to *"become sharers of the divine nature"* (*2 Peter* 1:4 NAB)! The only sane response to such a great salvation is overflowing joy and thanksgiving.

> With joy you will draw water from the wells of salvation. And you will say in that day: "Give thanks to the

LORD. . . . Shout, and sing for joy, O inhabitant of Zion, for great in your midst is the Holy One of Israel" (Isaiah 12:3-4, 6).

Salvation as we have said, is not of our own doing, but is a free gift from God. *"The grace of God has appeared for the salvation of all men" (Titus 2:12).*

The wages of sin is death, but the free gift of God is eternal life in Christ Jesus our Lord (Romans 6:23).

St. Paul makes it clear that there is no way we can earn salvation; there is no way we can be "good enough" to win God's approval. Rather, our salvation comes from Him as a gift:

For by grace you have been saved through faith; and this is not your own doing, it is the gift of God—not because of works, lest any man should boast (Ephesians 2:8-9).

But if it is by grace, it is no longer on the basis of works; otherwise grace would no longer be grace (Romans 11:6).

We must respond to this gift, either accepting it or refusing it. Through Jesus, the Father has extended His hand of welcome to us, inviting us back into the deepest love relationship with Himself. Will we accept His invitation? This is the topic of the rest of this book: what must I do to be saved? What must my response to God be?

Chapter 3

What Must I Do to be Saved?

We have emphasized that salvation comes from God as a free gift. He has taken the initiative; He has taken the risk. He has extended His mercy and forgiveness to us, and now He awaits our response. Will we take advantage of His good will toward us and return to Him, like the prodigal son?

> *"I tell you, there will likewise be more joy in heaven over one repentant sinner than over ninety-nine right-eous people who have no need to repent"* (*Luke* 15:7 NAB).

Or will we again spurn our Lover, rejecting the very One in whom our happiness lies? The bulk of this book is a selection of what the Scriptures teach us about our response to God's grace, what we must do to seize the salvation God has offered us.

The basic outline of how we say "yes" to God's invitation goes like this:

1) first, we must hear the good news;

2) the word we hear must have some appeal—it must "ring true," or "strike a chord" in the heart of the believer. "Yes! I've found it!" We receive it with joy;

3) long-term, there must be a profound change in the way we live, and our lives must bear fruit for God's kingdom.

What is the essence of this profound change in our lives? It is this. There has to be a shift in who is at the center of our lives. Picture your life as a kingdom with a throne in the center and servants around the throne awaiting the commands of the king. The servants are the various people and projects in our lives, the things and relationships that fill our lives. If we are honest, most of us must admit that we have enthroned ourselves as supreme lord of our own lives. The change that must take place is clear: we must get off the throne and allow Jesus to take His rightful place on the throne of our lives. Jesus is the King of kings and the Lord of lords; He is in charge. Our motto becomes, *"'Not my will, but thine, be done'"* (*Luke* 22:42).

> *I have been crucified with Christ, and the life I live now is not my own; Christ is living in me. I still live my human life, but it is a life of faith in the Son of God, who loved me and gave himself for me* (*Galatians* 2:19-20 NAB).

* * *

We saw in the quote from *Ephesians* 2:8-9 at the end of the preceding chapter that salvation is a free gift from God, received through faith. What is this faith through which we receive the grace of salvation?

> *Faith is confident assurance concerning what we hope for, and conviction about things we do not see* (*Hebrews* 11:1 NAB).

But is it enough for our whole being to cry out "Yes!" to the word of truth? Is it enough to say to ourselves (and to others), "This is what I believe"? Or is it our choices in life, how we act from day to day, which reveals our real "operating beliefs"? As we will see in more detail later when the Scriptures are allowed to speak for themselves, each of these aspects of faith is necessary. Sooner or later we must *"believe in our hearts"* (*Romans* 10:10), *"confess with our lips"* (*Romans* 10:10), and become *"doers of the word, not hearers only"* (*James* 1:22).

When Jesus began His preaching mission, He said, *"'Reform your lives and believe in the gospel!'"* (*Mark* 1:15 NAB).

1) Repent, that is, change the way we are living; 2) Believe what He says. Either one without the other is not enough. A true conversion to Jesus Christ involves both the inside and the outside of a person; both heart and hands must be given totally to the Lord. Heroic deeds without a change of heart (see *1 Corinthians* 13:1-3) are as useless as faith that does not bear fruit in action (see *James* 2:17). Furthermore, the inner change and the outer change reinforce each other:

> *Jesus then said to the Jews who had believed in him, "If you continue in my word, you are truly my disciples, and you will know the truth, and the truth will make you free" (John* 8:31-32).

Notice, Jesus was speaking to those who already believed in Him. He told them they would come to a deeper knowledge of the truth by remaining in His word. In turn, this deeper "knowing" of the truth would lead to new freedom, especially freedom from sin, as is clear from *John* 8:33-36.

To believe in Jesus and remain in His word, then, makes one a disciple. But a disciple is one who obeys His word, as we can see from the following quote: *"'Anyone who does not take up his cross and follow me cannot be my disciple.'"* (*Luke* 14:27 NAB). So, acting on the word leads to a deeper faith, and a deeper faith leads to acting on the word more freely.

The Scriptures in the rest of this book have been put more or less in the order indicated above: first, those which deal with the beginning of salvation—hearing the word, believing it, receiving baptism; then those which have to do with living a new life in Christ—obeying God's commands, following the lead of the Holy Spirit, praying, forgiving others; then those which have to do with growing and maturing in the love of Christ, putting on the character of Christ—dying to self, persevering over the long haul, growing in humility and love.

The dozens of Scriptures which follow build up a picture of the Christian life that is necessary for salvation. The idea is not to present a picture that is overwhelming ("oh, I could never do all that!"), but to present a picture that is complete.

Even though we have separated these Scriptures into many categories for ease of discussion, it is the whole picture we are aiming at. The Scriptures in all of the categories work together to tell one story—they are a unity. You will notice that many of the quotes overlap categories and could have been placed elsewhere. We could say these are the glue that binds the whole together.

A good way to take stock of our faith might be to see if any of these major areas are missing in our lives—perhaps a sign that our faith is lopsided or less than fully genuine. One or two little items missing are not alarming, but if a whole area is missing on a consistent basis, there may be good reason to take corrective action.

It is vitally important to realize that the context in which all of this takes place is a community context. No one of us is saved as an individual apart from the whole Christian family. We are all linked together as a very real body—the body of Christ. *"If one member suffers, all the members suffer with it; if one member is honored, all the members share its joy"* (*1 Corinthians* 12:26 NAB). This is more than empathy—we are one body!

Section 1

THE BEGINNING OF FAITH
Looking for Something

The beginning of faith both surrounds and lies within every human being. The awesomeness of creation raises questions:

> *When I behold your heavens, the work of your fingers, the moon and stars which you set in place—what is man that you should be mindful of him, or the son of man that you should care for him?* (*Psalm* 8:4-5 NAB).

> *But ask the beasts, and they will teach you; the birds of the air, and they will tell you; or the plants of the earth, and they will teach you; and the fish of the sea will declare to you. Who among all these does not know that the hand of the LORD has done this?* (*Job* 12:7-9).

> *Lift up your eyes on high and see: who created these? He who brings out their host by number, calling them all by name; by the greatness of his might, and because he is strong in power not one is missing* (*Isaiah* 40:26).

Not only do the wonders of the created world speak to us of an unseen Creator, but our own hearts testify that there is something more. In searching for this "something more," however, it is possible to wander off in directions away from the LORD. This is disastrous, unless we learn from our mistakes and finally find the true God. The author of *Ecclesiastes* seems to have followed all of the wrong paths he could think of before finding that they all reached a dead end:

And I applied my mind to search and investigate in wisdom all things that are done under the sun. . . . I thought of beguiling my senses with wine. . . . I undertook great works. . . . I amassed for myself silver and gold. . . . I got myself male and female singers and all human luxuries. . . . Behold! all was vanity and a chase after wind (Ecclesiastes 1:13, 2:3, 4, 8, 11 NAB).

All is vanity because we all must die:

[Man] shall see that even the wise die, the fool and the stupid alike must perish and leave their wealth to others. Their graves are their homes for ever, their dwelling places to all generations (Psalm 49:10-11).

By God's grace we may eventually discover that the paths which, on the surface seem to lead to happiness, in fact lead to death. But our hearts continue to whisper, "There is more!" Is there one path that is true? Can we ever hope to find it? St. Paul tells us that not only can we find God, we have no excuse if we don't find Him, since His stamp upon creation is clear:

What can be known about God is plain to [men], because God has shown it to them. Ever since the creation of the world his invisible nature, namely, his eternal power and deity, has been clearly perceived in the things that have been made. So they are without excuse (Romans 1:20).

Only those who do not want to find God will fail to find Him:

From one stock he made every nation of mankind to dwell on the face of the earth. . . . They were to grope for him and perhaps eventually to find him (Acts 17:26, 27 NAB).

God has planted an inner urging within us. Because we are made by Him, because we are like Him, we are drawn to Him:

God created man in his own image, in the image of God he created him (Genesis 1:27).

This yearning for God is expressed well by the Psalmists:

> *As the hind longs for the running waters, so my soul longs for you, O God. Athirst is my soul for God, the living God. When shall I go and behold the face of God? (Psalm 42:2-3 NAB).*

> *O God, thou art my God, I seek thee, my soul thirsts for thee; my flesh faints for thee, as in a dry and weary land where no water is (Psalm 63:1).*

The Lord has made a promise:

> *"Ask, and it will be given you; seek, and you will find; knock, and it will be opened to you. For every one who asks receives, and he who seeks finds, and to him who knocks it will be opened" (Matthew 7:7-8).*

> *You shall seek the LORD, your God; and you shall indeed find him when you search after him with your whole heart and your whole soul (Deuteronomy 4:29 NAB).*

Difficulty of Being Saved

After receiving assurance from God that we will find Him if we seek after Him with our whole being, it is important to emphasize "if we seek after Him with our whole being." Apparently we are likely to mislead ourselves on this point since Jesus has several words on the difficulty of being saved:

> *"Enter through the narrow gate. The gate that leads to damnation is wide, the road is clear, and many choose to travel it. But how narrow is the gate that leads to life, how rough the road, and how few there are who find it!" (Matthew 7:13-14 NAB).*

> *Someone asked him, "Lord, are they few in number who are to be saved?" He replied: "Try to come in through the narrow door. Many, I tell you, will try to enter and be unable" (Luke 13:23-24 NAB).*

In both of the above Scriptures Jesus says, "Try—strive." A better translation would be: "With everything you've got, make a great effort to enter by the narrow gate." Note, He does not directly answer the question, "Will many be saved?" but says, "*Try* to enter through the narrow gate." It is still a sobering response.

> *If the just man is saved only with difficulty, what is to become of the godless and the sinner?* (*1 Peter* 4:18 NAB).

> *Jesus said to them again, "Children, how hard it is to enter the kingdom of God! It is easier for a camel to go through the eye of a needle than for a rich man to enter the kingdom of God." And they were exceedingly astonished, and said to him, "Then who can be saved?" Jesus looked at them and said, "With men it is impossible, but not with God; for all things are possible with God"* (*Mark* 10:24-27).

Except for the free gift of God's grace, it is impossible for us to get into the kingdom of God. Praise be to God that it is His utmost desire to have mercy on us!

The Power of God's Word to Save

The word of God, whether spoken or written, has power, power to change our hearts.

> *The word of God is living and active, sharper than any two-edged sword, piercing to the division of soul and spirit, of joints and marrow, and discerning the thoughts and intentions of the heart* (*Hebrews* 4:12).

It has power because of its source—the word comes from the mouth of God.

> *For as the rain and the snow come down from heaven, and return not thither but water the earth, making it bring forth and sprout, giving seed to the sower and bread to the eater, so shall my word be that goes forth*

from my mouth; it shall not return to me empty, but it shall accomplish that which I purpose, and prosper in the thing for which I sent it (Isaiah 55:10-11).

God sent His word for our salvation, and His word is able to save us:

For the word of the cross is folly to those who are perishing, but to us who are being saved it is the power of God. . . . It pleased God through the folly of what we preach to save those who believe (1 Corinthians 1:18, 21).

I am not ashamed of the gospel: it is the power of God for salvation to every one who has faith (Romans 1:16).

Humbly welcome the word that has taken root in you, with its power to save you (James 1:21 NAB).

No less than an angel of the Lord told the centurion, Cornelius:

"'Send someone to Joppa and fetch Simon, known also as Peter. In the light of what he will tell you, you shall be saved, and all your household'" (Acts 11:13-14 NAB).

Not only can God's word bring us to the beginning stages of faith, but also to maturity:

From childhood you have been acquainted with the sacred writings which are able to instruct you for salvation through faith in Christ Jesus. All scripture is inspired by God and profitable for teaching, for reproof, for correction, and for training in righteousness, that the man of God may be complete, equipped for every good work (2 Timothy 3:15-17).

Yet can the word apart from The Word, Jesus Himself, bring salvation?

"You search the scriptures, because you think that in them you have eternal life; and it is they that bear witness to me; yet you refuse to come to me that you may have life" (John 5:39-40).

To this very day, when the old covenant is read the veil remains unlifted; it is only in Christ that it is taken away. Even now, when Moses is read a veil covers their understanding. "But whenever he turns to the Lord, the veil will be removed" (2 Corinthians 3:14-16 NAB).

Faith

We have already discussed what we mean by faith. By far the largest category of Scripture quotes are those which speak of salvation as a free gift of God that we receive through faith. Faith in what or in whom? The Scriptures are clear: it is faith in Jesus Christ and in the Gospel He proclaims which bring salvation.

The jailer asked Paul and Silas,

"Men, what must I do to be saved?" And they said, "Believe in the Lord Jesus, and you will be saved, you and your household" (Acts 16:30-31).

John gets to the heart of the matter in his Gospel:

"Yes, God so loved the world that he gave his only Son, that whoever believes in him may not die but may have eternal life. God did not send the Son into the world to condemn the world, but that the world might be saved through him. Whoever believes in him avoids condemnation, but whoever does not believe is already condemned for not believing in the name of God's only Son" (John 3:16-18 NAB).

In the parable of the sower and the seed, Jesus beautifully describes four types of heart-responses to the Gospel. He explains the first as follows:

"The seed is the word of God. The ones along the path are those who have heard; then the devil comes and takes away the word from their hearts, that they may not believe and be saved" (Luke 8:12-13).

From this last quote we see the beginning steps of faith: 1) hearing the word; 2) believing the word; 3) being saved.

We also see that we have an enemy, the devil, who tries to short-circuit the whole process at the very beginning by stealing the word from the hearts of those who have heard it before it has a chance to grow. It is sobering to realize that we have an enemy who is so full of malice that he tries to hurt God by working actively to keep His children from Him.

The following Scriptures show that faith, forgiveness, and love all lead to salvation. Jesus said to the woman who was a sinner who

> *wet his feet with her tears, and wiped them with the hair of her head, and kissed his feet, and anointed them with the ointment. . . . "Your sins are forgiven. . . . Your faith has saved you; go in peace" (Luke 7:38, 48, 50).*

To Simon, the Pharisee, who was judging the woman in his heart, Jesus said,

> *"I tell you, her sins, which are many, are forgiven, for she loved much; but he who is forgiven little, loves little" (Luke 7:47).*

No human initiative, no human action or ritual can save us:

> *For in Christ Jesus neither circumcision nor uncircumcision is of any avail, but faith working through love (Galatians 5:6).*

Baptism

Baptism is an immersion of the body in flowing water. Just as water cleanses the body, so baptism washes the soul from sin. It is an act of faith to believe that this spiritual cleansing takes place through the physical pouring of water.

The story of Naaman the Syrian may be an Old Testament version of baptism. Naaman traveled to the prophet Elisha in hopes of being cleansed of leprosy. Elisha told him to wash in the Jordan River:

He turned about in anger and left. But his servants came up and reasoned with him. "My father," they said, "if the prophet had told you to do something extraordinary, would you not have done it? All the more now, since he said to you, 'Wash and be clean,' should you do as he said." So Naaman went down and plunged into the Jordan seven times at the word of the man of God. His flesh became again like the flesh of a little child, and he was clean (2 Kings 5:12-14 NAB).

Immediately before Jesus' public life,

John the baptizer appeared in the wilderness, preaching a baptism of repentance for the forgiveness of sins. And there went out to him all the country of Judea, and all the people of Jerusalem; and they were baptized by him in the river Jordan, confessing their sins (Mark 1:4-5).

John was the most powerful prophetic figure in centuries. Expectations were high. Was he the Messiah? John told them:

"I baptize you in water for the sake of reform, but the one who will follow me is more powerful than I. I am not even fit to carry his sandals. He it is who will baptize you in the Holy Spirit and fire" (Matthew 3:11 NAB).

And *"then Jesus came from Galilee to the Jordan to John, to be baptized by him" (Matthew 3:13).* The Fathers of the Church teach that all the waters of the earth were sanctified when Jesus was baptized. From that moment on, everything was new!

Just before ascending to the right hand of the Father, Jesus commanded,

"Go therefore and make disciples of all nations, baptizing them in the name of the Father and of the Son and of the Holy Spirit" (Matthew 28:19).

In Mark's Gospel, Jesus' final instructions to His disciples include:

"He who believes and is baptized will be saved; but he who does not believe will be condemned" (Mark 16:16).

The definitive Scripture verse on the necessity of baptism for salvation is in the Gospel of John:

Jesus answered, "Truly, truly, I say to you, unless one is born of water and the Spirit, he cannot enter the kingdom of God" (John 3:5).

The Apostle Peter mentions the link between baptism and salvation by making an analogy to Noah's ark, in which

eight persons were saved through water. Baptism, which corresponds to this, now saves you, not as a removal of dirt from the body but as an appeal to God for a clear conscience, through the resurrection of Jesus Christ (1 Peter 3:20-21).

There are several examples in the *Acts of the Apostles* of baptism immediately following belief. This indicates that baptism is the normal response to belief in the Gospel.

After Peter's exhortation on the day of Pentecost, his hearers asked,

"What are we to do, brothers?" Peter answered: "You must reform and be baptized, each one of you, in the name of Jesus Christ, that your sins may be forgiven: then you will receive the gift of the Holy Spirit" (Acts 2:37-38 NAB).

But when they believed Philip as he preached good news about the kingdom of God and the name of Jesus Christ, they were baptized, both men and women (Acts 8:12).

Faith in Jesus Christ automatically brings us into relationship with other believers. We are not baptized as isolated individuals. When we are baptized into Christ, we are also baptized into His Body, the Church:

> *By one Spirit we were all baptized into one body—*
> *Jews or Greeks, slaves or free—and all were made to*
> *drink of one Spirit. For the body does not consist of*
> *one member but of many (1 Corinthians 12:13-14).*

Is it possible for one who is not baptized to be saved? St. Paul
suggests that it is:

> *When Gentiles who have not the law do by nature*
> *what the law requires, they are a law to themselves,*
> *even though they do not have the law. They show that*
> *what the law requires is written on their hearts, while*
> *their conscience also bears witness and their conflict-*
> *ing thoughts accuse them or perhaps excuse them on*
> *that day when, according to my gospel, God judges*
> *the secrets of men by Christ Jesus (Romans 2:14-16).*

* * *

As indicated in the Scriptures, the Catholic Church considers
Baptism to be the gateway to salvation. As the water is poured
over the baptized, every sin is "washed away" and the Holy
Spirit rushes in, making him a new creation in Jesus.

Baptism is normally absolutely necessary for salvation. But if a
person who desires (or would desire) Baptism is not able to be baptized, either because of ignorance or death, we are confident that
God is able to pour out His saving grace anyway. Baptism is seen as
so essential to salvation that we even make sure to baptize infants,
drawing on the faith of the parents and of the whole Church.

The Catholic Church teaches that the grace of Baptism is completed or perfected by Confirmation. In Confirmation, our bond
with Christ and His Church is strengthened and deepened by the
Holy Spirit, and we are better equipped to live the faith and
spread the Gospel:

> *Now when the apostles at Jerusalem heard that*
> *Samaria had received the word of God, they sent to*
> *them Peter and John, who came down and prayed for*

*them that they might receive the Holy Spirit; for it had
not yet fallen on any of them, but they had only been
baptized in the name of the Lord Jesus. Then they laid
their hands on them and they received the Holy Spirit
(Acts 8:14-17).*

The outward signs of Confirmation are the anointing of the
forehead with perfumed oil and the laying on of hands, both signifying the Holy Spirit.

The LORD, speaking of David, said to Samuel:

*"There—anoint him, for this is he!" Then Samuel,
with the horn of oil in hand, anointed him in the midst
of his brothers; and from that day on, the spirit of the
LORD rushed upon David (1 Samuel 16:12-13 NAB).*

* * *

Baptism and Confirmation are both sacraments. What is a
sacrament? *The Catechism of the Catholic Church* (#1131)
teaches that a sacrament is:

- an effective sign of grace
- instituted by Christ
- entrusted to the Church
- gives divine life
- draws on the power of Jesus' Paschal mystery
- a visible rite which makes present the graces it signifies

The anointing of the Holy Spirit flowing over the Head (Jesus)
runs down over the whole Body (see *Psalm* 133) and then over
the whole creation, making them sacred. Ever since the Word of
God became flesh, grace has been breaking through into our
world by means of the signs given to us by Jesus. A sacrament is
a visible sign, something that can be seen, touched, tasted, or
smelled. It is something tangible, incarnational. A sacrament con-
sists of signs and symbols, words and actions using materials
such as water, oil, bread, and wine.

The very act of celebrating the rite makes present the grace of each sacrament regardless of the personal holiness of either the minister or the recipient. However, an adult recipient must receive the sacrament with the proper dispositions for it to be effective and fruitful. He can place no obstacle in the way of the grace flowing from the sacrament. First, he must intend to receive the grace of the sacrament. Further, the attitude of his heart must be open to receiving God's grace. The sacraments are not magic; they must be received in faith, just as it was an act of faith for Naaman to plunge himself into the Jordan. The recipient must have an attitude of co-operating with the grace received, intending to increase in faith and love, hoping to become more and more like Jesus in character.

The sign of each sacrament corresponds to the grace given; that is, when we pour water in Baptism our souls are cleansed from sin, and when we eat the bread and wine of the Eucharist Jesus feeds us with His Body and Blood, and so on.

Jesus also gave other signs, such as the washing of feet, which are like the sacraments. Guided by the inspiration of the Holy Spirit, however, the Church has discerned over the ages that there are seven sacraments: Baptism, Confirmation, Penance, Eucharist, Holy Orders, Matrimony, and the Anointing of the Sick. Even though there are many other signs, some performed by Jesus in the Gospels and some not, which can be vehicles for grace, only these seven are sacraments. The others we call sacramentals. The Church teaches that the sacraments are necessary for salvation. In this book we have demonstrated this from the Scriptures for several of the sacraments individually.

Just as our natural life is marked by significant times—birth, death, and marriage or other vocational choice—so is our spiritual life. The sacraments of initiation, Baptism, Confirmation, and Eucharist accompany us in our spiritual birth. The sacraments of healing, Penance and the Anointing of the Sick are for the times we are physically or spiritually sick or dying. The sacraments in the service of communion, Matrimony and Holy Orders, are there to sanctify our choice of vocation in life, our choice of how we will bring Jesus' love to others.

Some of the sacramentals, besides washing of feet, are: the sign of the cross, containing the central mysteries of the faith, the mystery of the Most Holy Trinity, and the mystery of the cross; holy water, a reminder of the water of the new birth of Baptism; blessed oil, a sign of anointing of priests, prophets, and kings, and also a sign of healing as a divine medicinal balm; laying on of hands, a sign of the giving of the Holy Spirit; blessed candles, signifying the Light of Christ; blessed objects of all kinds; blessings of persons, and many others.

Truth

As we saw in *Acts* 2:38 above, every baptized person has received the Holy Spirit, Who is the Spirit of truth.

> *"When the Spirit of truth comes, he will guide you into all the truth"* (*John* 16:13).

Another word for truth is *reality*. The truth we are speaking of here is the truth based on knowing Jesus, Who is the Truth, Who is the ultimate Reality. We know this kind of truth when we encounter it, because an inner witness, the Holy Spirit, has convinced us in our hearts. The Spirit of truth is the Spirit of Jesus, for Jesus has said,

> *"I am the way, and the truth, and the life"* (*John* 14:6).

If we receive His truth we will be saved:

> *Jesus then went on to say to those Jews who believed in him: "If you live according to my teaching, you are truly my disciples; then you will know the truth, and the truth will set you free"* (*John* 8:31-32 NAB).

St. Paul emphatically states:

> *In [Christ] you too were chosen; when you heard the glad tidings of salvation, the word of truth, and believed in it, you were sealed with the Holy Spirit who had been promised. He is the pledge of our inher-*

> *itance, the first payment against the full redemption of*
> *a people God has made his own, to praise his glory*
> (*Ephesians* 1:13-14 NAB).

If one believes the word of truth, he will be saved; if one does not believe the truth, but a lie, he will not be saved:

> *The coming of the lawless one by the activity of*
> *Satan will be with all power and with pretended*
> *signs and wonders, and with all wicked deception*
> *for those who are to perish, because they refused to*
> *love the truth and so be saved. Therefore God sends*
> *upon them a strong delusion, to make them believe*
> *what is false, so that all may be condemned who did*
> *not believe the truth but had pleasure in unright-*
> *eousness. But we are bound to give thanks to God*
> *always for you, brethren beloved by the Lord,*
> *because God chose you from the beginning to be*
> *saved, through sanctification by the Spirit and belief*
> *in the truth* (*2 Thessalonians* 2:9-13).

God our Savior *"desires all men to be saved and to come to the knowledge of the truth"* (*1 Timothy* 2:4). Further, St. Paul instructs us: *"Let us profess the truth in love and grow to the full maturity of Christ the head"* (*Ephesians* 4:15 NAB).

Profess, *live* the truth in love. We must have both: truth without love is not the Truth; love without truth is not Love. The proof of this? Jesus is Truth (*John* 14:6). Jesus, being God, is Love (*1 John* 4:16). Jesus, being God, is One and cannot be divided (see, for instance, *John* 5:18, *John* 10:35-38 and *Deuteronomy* 6:4).

Acknowledge My Sin

Part of the truth is that we have all sinned. Before we can turn away from sin, we have to recognize we have done evil in God's sight and admit it:

As long as I would not speak, my bones wasted away with my groaning all the day, for day and night your hand was heavy upon me; my strength was dried up as by the heat of summer. Then I acknowledged my sin to you, my guilt I covered not. I said, "I confess my faults to the LORD," and you took away the guilt of my sin (Psalm 32:3-5 NAB).

If we say, "We are free from the guilt of sin," we deceive ourselves; the truth is not to be found in us. But if we acknowledge our sins, he who is just can be trusted to forgive our sins and cleanse us from every wrong (1 John 1:8-9 NAB).

Not only must we confess our sins to God; it is good to acknowledge our sins to our Christian brothers and sisters. In *James 5:16* we read: *"Therefore confess your sins to one another, and pray for one another, that you may be healed."* The Bible also tells us that sooner or later the truth becomes known whether we confess it or not:

"Nothing is covered up that will not be revealed, or hidden that will not be known" (Luke 12:2).

It is better that we see the truth about our own sins so we can do something about them than for everybody but us to know about them.

Contrition and Repentance

Contrition is a sorrow for our sins, a sorrow deep enough that we want to change the way we live. It is a true change of heart, not lip service.

Godly grief produces a repentance that leads to salvation and brings no regret, but worldly grief produces death (2 Corinthians 7:10).

Job was seized with this kind of sorrow when he encountered God in the whirlwind:

*I had heard of thee by the hearing of the ear, but now
my eye sees thee; therefore I despise myself, and
repent in dust and ashes (Job 42:5-6).*

King David was filled with grief when the prophet Nathan
came to him after his sin with Bathsheba. He realized that "*the
sacrifice acceptable to God is a broken spirit; a broken and contrite heart, O God, thou wilt not despise*" (*Psalm* 51:17).

St. Peter was saved from the depths of despair by a look of
love from Jesus:

*Peter responded, "My friend, I do not know what you
are talking about." At the very moment he was saying
this, a cock crowed. The Lord turned around and
looked at Peter, and Peter remembered the word that
the Lord had spoken to him, "Before the cock crows
today you will deny me three times." He went out and
wept bitterly (Luke 22:60-62 NAB).*

Repentance is the actual change of the way I live, turning
away from sin and turning toward God:

*When the righteous turns from his righteousness, and
commits iniquity, he shall die for it. And when the
wicked turns from his wickedness, and does what is
lawful and right, he shall live by it (Ezekiel 33:18-19).*

*Let the wicked forsake his way, and the unrighteous
man his thoughts; let him return to the LORD, that he
may have mercy on him, and to our God, for he will
abundantly pardon (Isaiah 55:7).*

No feelings of sorrow, however deep, bring salvation unless
accompanied by real changes in our lives. John the Baptist
warned the multitudes that came out to him:

*"Give some evidence that you mean to reform. . . .
Every tree that is not fruitful will be cut down and
thrown into the fire" (Luke 3:8, 9 NAB).*

* * *

In the Catholic Church, we distinguish between initial conversion, contrition and repentance, and subsequent need (after Baptism) for conversion, contrition, and repentance. After Baptism, we are still all too prone to sin, even seriously. The ordinary means for seeking reconciliation with God and the Church after Baptism is through the sacrament of Reconciliation or Penance. None of the other sacraments (except Baptism and in some circumstances, the Anointing of the Sick) can be worthily received without first confessing all mortal sins in the sacrament of Penance.

Mortal sin is serious business. Three conditions must be met for a sin to be so lethal as to destroy the life of the soul. 1) The sin must objectively be seriously wrong; that is, a violation of the Ten Commandments; 2) the person must have full knowledge of the seriousness of the action; 3) the person must freely and fully consent to the sinful action, knowing how wrong it is.

The sacrament of Penance was instituted by Jesus on the evening of the resurrection.

> *Jesus came and stood among them and said to them, "Peace be with you. . . ." And when he said this, he breathed on them, and said to them, "Receive the Holy Spirit. If you forgive the sins of any, they are forgiven; if you retain the sins of any, they are retained"* (*John* 20:19, 22-23).

In the sacrament of Penance, the penitent, full of sorrow for his offenses against God and his brothers and sisters, confesses his sins to a priest. The priest, representing both Jesus and the Church, applies the healing balm of God's forgiveness, mercifully and justly. To repair the damage to the sinner's oneness with himself, with God and with neighbor, the priest imposes an appropriate penance.

God cannot forgive us unless we are contrite of heart.

Contrition is sorrow for one's sins, hatred for them, and the resolution never to sin again. Without true conversion of the heart, no sins can be forgiven. *"Therefore, I tell you, her sins, which are many, are forgiven, for she loved much'"* (*Luke* 7:47).

The penitent should prepare for the sacrament of Penance by making an examination of conscience. The *Catechism of the Catholic Church* (#1454) recommends basing our examination of conscience on the following Scriptures: *Matthew* ch. 5-7, the Sermon on the Mount; *Romans* ch. 12-15; *1 Corinthians* ch. 12-13; *Galatians* ch. 5; *Ephesians* ch. 4-6.

Even though it is strictly necessary to receive the sacrament of Reconciliation only when in mortal sin, it is strongly recommended to confess regularly, at least monthly. This bears fruit in continually deeper conversion to Jesus Christ, making us more and more effective bearers of the Gospel to the world around us.

$$* \quad * \quad *$$

The sacrament of the Anointing of the Sick also removes sin. This sacrament is appropriate whenever one is in danger of death due to sickness or old age. It finds its foundation in the following Scripture:

> *Is any among you sick? Let him call for the elders of the church, and let them pray over him, anointing him with oil in the name of the Lord; and the prayer of faith will save the sick man, and the Lord will raise him up; and if he has committed sins, he will be forgiven* (*James* 5:14-15).

It is Jesus Who heals in the sacrament, perhaps physically, certainly spiritually. The sick person is given the grace to suffer with peace and courage, uniting his suffering with the saving work of Jesus' Passion. This offering of one's suffering in love for the sake of others brings benefit to the one offering and to the whole Body of Christ. The sick person, should he not be healed physically, is prepared for passing over to eternal life.

The sacramental sign is the anointing of the forehead and hands of the sick person with oil. The meaning of the anointing with oil becomes clearer when we recall that olive oil was considered to have medicinal qualities in New Testament times (recall the Good Samaritan who poured oil and wine on the wounds of the man who had been beaten—see *Luke* 10:34).

On Fire with Love for Him

When we first come to the Lord in faith, He fills us with a new fire and a new love that we are sure will never fade.

> *[They] welcomed the message with great enthusiasm.*
> *Each day they studied the Scriptures to see whether*
> *these things were so (Acts 17:11 NAB).*

As part of the conversion process, we may be struck with sorrow at how we have offended God. This deeply felt sorrow is then translated into fiery zeal to live for God:

> *See what earnestness this godly grief has produced in*
> *you, what eagerness to clear yourselves, what indig-*
> *nation, what alarm, what longing, what zeal, what*
> *punishment! (2 Corinthians 7:11).*

But it is possible for the fire of youth to slowly ebb away. Jesus chided the Church at Ephesus for exactly this reason:

> *"I know you are enduring patiently and bearing up for*
> *my name's sake, and you have not grown weary. But I*
> *have this against you, that you have abandoned the*
> *love you had at first. Remember then from what you*
> *have fallen, repent and do the works you did at first. If*
> *not, I will come to you and remove your lampstand*
> *from its place, unless you repent" (Revelation 2:3-5).*

A fire, whether a tiny candle flame or a raging forest fire, is a fire. Every fire has a burning intensity, producing heat and light. Jesus' own Heart is burning with love for us. If our love cannot be described as fiery, do we love at all? Judge from Jesus' words to the Church at Laodicea:

> *"I know your works: you are neither cold nor hot. Would that you were cold or hot! So, because you are lukewarm, and neither cold nor hot, I will spew you out of my mouth" (Revelation 3:15-16).*

Because we have this tendency to cool off with the passing of time, we have to take steps to fan the fire of our love. St. Paul exhorts the young man Timothy: *"I remind you to rekindle the gift of God that is within you" (2 Timothy 1:6).*

St. Peter is aware of the power of constantly calling to mind the basics of our faith to re-fire us:

> *I intend to recall these things to you constantly, even though you already understand and are firmly rooted in the truth you possess. I consider it my duty, as long as I live, to prompt you with this reminder (2 Peter 1:12-13 NAB).*

Without fire from the beginning to the end of the Christian life, our love dwindles and grows cold, and we are in danger of arriving at the end of our lives with no taste for the "Love Who is not loved":

> *We desire each one of you to show the same earnestness in realizing the full assurance of hope until the end, so that you may not be sluggish, but imitators of those who through faith and patience inherit the promises (Hebrews 6:11).*

> *Never flag in zeal, be aglow with the Spirit, serve the Lord (Romans 12:11).*

Life and Death Combat

Several scriptures refer to entering the kingdom of God by force or combat:

"From the days of John the Baptist until now the king-dom of heaven has suffered violence, and men of vio-lence take it by force" (Matthew 11:12).

"The law and the prophets were in force until John. From his time on, the good news of God's kingdom has been proclaimed, and people of every sort are forcing their way in" (Luke 16:16 NAB).

Fight the good fight of faith. Take firm hold on the everlasting life to which you were called (1 Timothy 6:12 NAB).

This seems to go beyond zeal or fire—the spiritual life is a combat. We are in a life and death war with enemies who are out to shame, degrade, and kill us. We can distinguish three foes in this war: the desires of our own flesh, the lure of the world, and the devil. We must wage a ferocious fight, wielding the weapons of light, with each of them.

We have tendencies within us toward both good and evil. The tendency toward evil is often called "the flesh" in the Scriptures:

Beloved, I beseech you. . . . to abstain from the pas-sions of the flesh that wage war against your soul (1 Peter 2:11).

Each person is tempted when he is lured and enticed by his own desire. Then desire when it has conceived gives birth to sin; and sin when it is full-grown brings forth death (James 1:14-15).

As with all spiritual battles, we are more likely to be success-ful in this one the sooner we resist the enemy: the best strategy is to "nip it in the bud."

The world, that is the part of our culture which is opposed to the Gospel of Jesus Christ, surrounds us with a continual invita-tion to sin. It is a sort of peer-pressure that conspires with our fleshly desires to lead us away from God. We must fight it with all our strength:

> *Do you not know that friendship with the world is enmity with God? Therefore whoever wishes to be a friend of the world makes himself an enemy of God (James 4:4).*

> *If any one loves the world, love for the Father is not in him. For all that is in the world, the lust of the flesh and the lust of the eyes and the pride of life, is not of the Father but is of the world (1 John 2:15-16).*

Besides being tempted to sin by the world, we are hated by the world and can expect to be persecuted by those who are of the world:

> *If you were of the world, the world would love its own; but because you are not of the world, but I chose you out of the world, therefore the world hates you. . . . If they persecuted me, they will persecute you (John 15:19, 20).*

In addition we have a mortal enemy in Satan, a fallen angel, who with cunning and power deliberately does everything he can to destroy us. As we see in the *Book of Job,* the devil has power to afflict us physically and emotionally, whether as individuals or whole societies:

> *"The thief comes only to steal and kill and destroy" (John 10:10).*

His most effective weapon, however, is not brute power, but deceit. He is the master of illusion and lies, able to make evil compellingly attractive:

> *"[The devil] was a murderer from the beginning, and has nothing to do with the truth, because there is no truth in him. When he lies, he speaks according to his own nature, for he is a liar and the father of lies" (John 8:44).*

We must hold fast to the truth in its purity to deflate the temptations of the devil. If we have committed our lives to Jesus and His kingdom of light, we are safe from the malice and snares of

Satan and his devils:

> *Put on the whole armor of God, that you may be able to stand against the wiles of the devil. For we are not contending against flesh and blood, but against the principalities, against the powers, against the world rulers of this present darkness, against the spiritual hosts of wickedness in the heavenly places* (*Ephesians* 6:11-12).

Single Hearted

Fervent love is always focused on the beloved in a total way. One who is divided is not in love:

> *"No man can serve two masters. He will either hate one and love the other or be attentive to one and despise the other"* (*Matthew* 6:24 NAB).

> *For that person must not suppose that a double-minded man, unstable in all his ways, will receive anything from the Lord* (*James* 1:7-8).

> *Whoever wishes to be a friend of the world makes himself an enemy of God. . . . Submit yourselves therefore to God. Resist the devil and he will flee from you. Draw near to God and he will draw near to you. Cleanse your hands, you sinners, and purify your hearts, you men of double mind* (*James* 4:4, 7-8).

Jesus Himself was always focused on His Father, always of one heart: *"For the Son of God, Jesus Christ. . . . was not Yes and No; but in him it is always Yes"* (*2 Corinthians* 1:19).

He taught us to be like Him:

> *"Blest are the single-hearted; for they shall see God"* (*Matthew* 5:8 NAB).

> *"Whoever puts his hand to the plow but keeps looking back is unfit for the reign of God"* (*Luke* 9:62 NAB).

Whenever the treasure of our hearts is someone or something other than the Lord, we are engaging in a form of idol worship:

> *"He who loves father or mother more than me is not worthy of me; and he who loves son or daughter more than me is not worthy of me"* (*Matthew* 10:37).

We would do well to heed King David's advice to his son, Solomon:

> *"Know the God of your father, and serve him with a whole heart and with a willing mind; for the LORD searches all hearts, and understands every plan and thought. If you seek him, he will be found by you; but if you forsake him, he will cast you off for ever"* (*1 Chronicles* 28:9).

The Body and Blood of Christ

After Jesus' disciples had been with Him for a time, He said to them:

> *"I am the living bread which came down from heaven; if any one eats of this bread, he will live for ever; and the bread which I shall give for the life of the world is my flesh."* The Jews then disputed among themselves, saying, "How can this man give us his flesh to eat?" (*John* 6:51-52).

Jesus did not retract His statement, but intensified it. He said to them,

> *"Truly, truly, I say to you, unless you eat the flesh of the Son of man and drink his blood, you have no life in you; he who eats my flesh and drinks my blood has eternal life. . . ."* Many of his disciples, when they heard it, said, "This is a hard saying; who can listen to it" (*John* 6:53-54, 60).

Faced with the possibility of losing many of those who had been following Him, Jesus did not take back His words, but rather commented,

> *"There are some of you that do not believe. . . ." After this many of his disciples drew back and no longer went about with him (John 6:64, 66).*

Jesus did not run after them, trying to clear up a misunderstanding over words. Rather, Jesus said to the twelve, " 'Do you want to leave me too?' " (*John* 6:67 NAB).

At the last supper Jesus revealed the mystery of His Body and Blood:

> *During the meal Jesus took bread, blessed it, broke it, and gave it to his disciples. "Take this and eat it," he said, "this is my body." Then he took a cup, gave thanks, and gave it to them. "All of you must drink from it," he said, "For this is my blood, the blood of the covenant, to be poured out in behalf of many for the forgiveness of sins" (Matthew 26:26-28 NAB).*

St. Paul, in a teaching contrasting true and false worship, asks,

> *Is not the cup of blessing we bless a sharing in the blood of Christ? And is not the bread we break a sharing in the body of Christ? (1 Corinthians 10:16 NAB).*

The great importance that the early Christians gave to the "breaking of the bread" is clear from another teaching of St. Paul:

> *Whoever eats the bread or drinks the cup of the Lord unworthily sins against the body and blood of the Lord (1 Corinthians 11:27 NAB).*

Section 2

NEW LIFE IN CHRIST
Seek the Lord

In the section "Looking for Something" we discussed the search for "something more" that can lead to discovering God. In this section we are looking at a different group of searchers, namely, those who already have some knowledge of God who are crying out to Him, reaching to Him for help.

Whoever would draw near to God must believe that he exists and that he rewards those who seek him (*Hebrews* 11:6).

For those who seek Him in faith, there is a promise from God: " *'Every one who calls upon the name of the Lord will be saved' "* (*Romans* 10:13). Further, the LORD exhorts us to seek Him:

For thus says the LORD to the house of Israel: "Seek me, that you may live" (Amos 5:4 NAB).

Sow for yourselves righteousness, reap the fruit of steadfast love; break up your fallow ground, for it is time to seek the LORD, that he may come and rain salvation upon you (Hosea 10:12).

All you who are thirsty, come to the water! You who have no money, come receive grain and eat; come, without paying and without cost, drink wine and milk! . . . Come to me heedfully, listen, that you may have life. I will renew with you the everlasting covenant (Isaiah 55:1, 3 NAB).

We see from the following quote that sincere seeking carries with it a willingness to reform one's life:

> *Seek the LORD while he may be found, call him while he is near. Let the scoundrel forsake his way, and the wicked man his thoughts; let him turn to the LORD for mercy; to our God, who is generous in forgiving* (*Isaiah* 55:6-7 NAB).

We can almost taste the passion of God as He continually invites us, even begs us, to come to Him:

> *On the last day of the feast, the great day, Jesus stood up and proclaimed, "If any one thirst, let him come to me and drink"* (*John* 7:37).

Those who seek after the LORD have cause for rejoicing:

> *May all who seek thee rejoice and be glad in thee; may those who love thy salvation say continually, "Great is the LORD"* (*Psalm* 40:16).

Fear the Lord

No one who has had an encounter with the living God is ever the same afterwards. The awesomeness of God's presence brings new light; we see more truly who we are, and more truly who God is. We have a new eagerness to please Him.

When the profound goodness of God's blessings sinks in we are filled with wonder. Peter had just such an overwhelming experience of God's power when he and his companions made the great catch of fish at Jesus' command:

> *When Simon Peter saw it, he fell down at Jesus' knees, saying "Depart from me, for I am a sinful man, O Lord." For he was astonished, and all that were with him, at the catch of fish which they had taken* (*Luke* 5:8-9).

The Scriptures speak of the many benefits God gives to those who fear Him. Salvation is primary among these:

> *He fulfills the desire of all who fear him, he also hears their cry, and saves them (Psalm 145:19).*

> *The fear of the LORD is a fountain of life, that one may avoid the snares of death (Proverbs 14:27).*

One who has no fear of the LORD has no real knowledge of Him, has never encountered Him, and therefore cannot be saved by Him. Fear of the LORD is a sign that we are capable of receiving salvation:

> *Brethren, sons of the family of Abraham, and those among you that fear God, to us has been sent the message of this salvation (Acts 13:26).*

To the extent that we tremble before God's presence, to that extent we are in touch with reality. A healthy fear of the LORD inclines us to obey Him:

> *Therefore, my beloved, as you have always obeyed, so now, not only as in my presence but much more in my absence, work out your own salvation with fear and trembling (Philippians 2:12).*

Even Jesus gave God the Father this respect, and it led to His own salvation from death:

> *In the days of his flesh, Jesus offered up prayers and supplications with loud cries and tears, to him who was able to save him from death, and he was heard for his godly fear (Hebrews 5:7).*

Fear of the Lord comes from realizing exactly Who He is; profound worship is our natural and immediate response. Therefore, *"Let us offer to God acceptable worship, with reverence and awe; for our God is a consuming fire" (Hebrews 12:28-29).*

Jesus does not want us to live in fear. The only exception to this is a healthy fear of God. This is not fear that God is looking for an excuse to smash us (because if God is looking for any excuse for us, it is an excuse to have mercy on us), but awe and reverence, being overwhelmed by Love.

> *"I tell you, my friends, do not fear those who kill the body, and after that have no more that they can do. But I will warn you whom to fear: fear him who, after he has killed, has power to cast into hell; yes, I tell you, fear him"* (Luke 12:4-5).

Worship the Lord

Fear of the Lord leads directly into reverential worship of God. This happened on a couple of occasions when the disciples' boat was being swamped by high seas:

> *[Jesus] stood up and took the winds and the sea to task. Complete calm ensued; the men were dumbfounded. "What sort of man is this," they said, "that even the winds and the sea obey him?"* (Matthew 8:26-27 NAB).

> *And when they got into the boat, the wind ceased. And those in the boat worshiped him, saying, "Truly you are the Son of God"* (Matthew 14:32-33).

It is necessary to worship God, and Him alone, in order to be saved. For Jesus has made it clear that we must obey all of God's commands to be saved:

> *One came up to him, saying "Teacher, what good deed must I do, to have eternal life?" And he said to him, . . . "If you would enter life, keep the commandments"* (Matthew 19:16, 17).

In particular, responding to the temptation of the devil, Jesus answered him, *"It is written, 'You shall worship the Lord your God, and him only shall you serve'"* (Luke 4:8). Our worship must consist in more than empty ritual. God is looking for worship from the heart. As Jesus said to the woman at the well,

*"The hour is coming, and now is, when the true wor-
shipers will worship the Father in spirit and truth, for
such the Father seeks to worship him. God is spirit,
and those who worship him must worship in spirit and
truth" (John 4:23-24).*

* * *

Catholics believe that worship of God is a serious obligation.
We set aside Sunday, the Lord's day, as a day devoted to worship
of God, to spiritual restoration and bodily rest, a day to build the
family. For a Catholic to miss the Holy Sacrifice of the Mass on
Sunday without a good reason is a serious matter, calling into
question one's relationship with God:

> *Let us consider how to stir up one another to love and
> good works, not neglecting to meet together, as is the
> habit of some, but encouraging one another, and all the
> more as you see the Day drawing near (Hebrews 10:25).*

Although there are many ways to worship God, individually
and communally, spontaneously and ritually, the Second Vatican
Council teaches that the public worship of the Church, especially
the Mass, is both the goal for which we aim and the source of the
Church's power (see *The Catholic Catechism* #1074).

Obedience

As we saw above, fear of the LORD leads us immediately and
naturally to obey God. This obedience to God's will, especially as
expressed in His commandments, is necessary to our salvation:

> *Not every one who says to me, "Lord, Lord," shall
> enter the kingdom of heaven, but he who does the will
> of my Father who is in heaven. On that day many will
> say to me, "Lord, Lord, did we not prophesy in your
> name, and cast out demons in your name, and do
> many mighty works in your name?" And then will I
> declare to them, "I never knew you; depart from me,
> you evildoers" (Matthew 7:21-22).*

> *He who believes in the Son has eternal life; he who*
> *does not obey the Son shall not see life, but the wrath*
> *of God rests upon him (John 3:36).*

It is not enough to appreciate God's command and to think that
it is a good idea:

> *For it is not the hearers of the law who are righteous*
> *before God, but the doers of the law who will be justi-*
> *fied (Romans 2:13).*

St. Paul states that we have no choice but to be obedient
slaves—but to whom? To God or to sin? Our choice between
these two masters has eternal consequences:

> *Do you not know that if you yield yourselves to any*
> *one as obedient slaves, you are slaves of the one*
> *whom you obey, either of sin, which leads to death, or*
> *of obedience, which leads to righteousness? . . . Now*
> *that you have been set free from sin and have become*
> *slaves of God, the return you get is sanctification and*
> *its end, eternal life (Romans 6:16, 22).*

The author of the *Letters to the Hebrews,* writing of Jesus says,

> *Son though he was, he learned obedience from what*
> *he suffered; and when perfected, he became the source*
> *of eternal salvation for all who obey him (Hebrews*
> *5:8-9 NAB).*

In the following verses we see how beautifully truth, intimate
knowledge of God, obedience, and love combine for our salvation:

> *The man who claims, "I have known him," without*
> *keeping his commandments, is a liar; in such a one*
> *there is no truth. But whoever keeps his word, truly*
> *has the love of God been made perfect in him. The*
> *way we can be sure we are in union with him is for the*
> *man who claims to abide in him to conduct himself*
> *just as he did (1 John 2:4-6 NAB).*

There is an extraordinary verse later in John's letter which indicates that we ought to obey God with delight, finding it a joy to do His will:

> *The love of God consists in this: that we keep his com-*
> *mandments—and his commandments are not burden-*
> *some (1 John 5:3 NAB).*

This is echoed by the Psalmist: *"Blessed is the man who fears the LORD, who greatly delights in his commandments!" (Psalm 112:1).*

Obedience to God extends to obedience to those who are in positions of authority over us.

> *Let every person be subject to the governing authori-*
> *ties. For there is no authority except from God, and*
> *those that exist have been instituted by God. Therefore*
> *he who resists the authorities resists what God has*
> *appointed (Romans 13:1-2).*

This submission to human authorities includes those who are cruel and unjust; it urges us to respect all men, those we love and those we don't:

> *Because of the Lord, be obedient to every human insti-*
> *tution, whether to the emperor as sovereign or to the*
> *governors he commissions. . . . You must esteem the*
> *person of every man. Foster love for the brothers, rev-*
> *erence for God, respect for the emperor. You house-*
> *hold slaves, obey your masters with all deference, not*
> *only the good and reasonable ones but even those who*
> *are harsh. . . . You married women must obey your*
> *husbands. . . . You husbands, too, must show consider-*
> *ation for those who share your lives (1 Peter 2:13-14,*
> *17-18, 3:1, 7 NAB).*

The tone of this obedience is not begrudging ("well, okay, if I *have* to") but a loving service, a laying down of one's own will for the sake of others: *"Be subject to one another out of rever-ence for Christ" (Ephesians 5:21).*

Following the Lead of the Holy Spirit

In addition to the law written in stone there is the law of the Spirit of God written on our hearts (see *2 Corinthians* 3:3). If we are to be fully obedient to Him, we must obey the promptings of the Holy Spirit as well as the written commandments.

The whisperings of the Spirit must be discerned before we act on them; they can never contradict the written law. Rather the Holy Spirit teaches us how to custom-fit the law of Love to our own personal situation:

> *Do not quench the Spirit, and do not despise prophesy-ing, but test everything; hold fast what is good, abstain from every form of evil (1 Thessalonians 5:19-22).*

One who has been born anew by water and the Holy Spirit is indwelt by the Holy Spirit. *"You know him, for he dwells with you, and will be in you" (John 14:17).*

One who is filled with the Holy Spirit is led by the Holy Spirit. Immediately after being baptized by John, *"Jesus was led up by the Spirit into the wilderness to be tempted by the devil" (Matthew 4:1).* Not only Jesus, but *"all who are led by the Spirit of God are sons of God" (Romans 8:14)* although we are sons by adoption. To be saved we must follow the lead of the Spirit. It is a choice between following the Holy Spirit or the desires of the flesh:

> *My point is that you should live in accord with the Spirit and you will not yield to the cravings of the flesh. The flesh lusts against the Spirit and the Spirit against the flesh; the two are directly opposed. . . . Those who belong to Christ Jesus have crucified their flesh with its passions and desires. Since we live by the Spirit, let us follow the Spirit's lead (Galatians 5:16-17, 24-25 NAB).*

We can tell the difference between what is of the flesh and what is of the Holy Spirit by the fruits they produce: *"to set the mind on the flesh is death, but to set the mind on the Spirit is life and peace" (Romans 8:6).* And *"the written law kills, but the Spirit gives life"*

(*2 Corinthians* 3:6 NAB).

St. Paul assures us that the difference is nothing less than the difference between eternal life and death:

> *Do not be deceived; God is not mocked, for whatever a man sows, that he will also reap. For he who sows to his own flesh will from the flesh reap corruption; but he who sows to the Spirit will from the Spirit reap eternal life* (*Galatians* 6:7-8).

Good Works

As we have indicated above, good works also have a place in whether we are saved. For when Jesus, the King, comes in His glory, he will separate sheep from goats:

> *"The king will say to those on his right: 'Come. You have my Father's blessing! Inherit the kingdom prepared for you from the creation of the world. For I was hungry and you gave me food, I was thirsty and you gave me drink. I was a stranger and you welcomed me, naked and you clothed me, in prison and you came to visit me.'"* (*Matthew* 25:34-36 NAB).

> *"Then he will say to those on his left: 'Out of my sight, you condemned, into that everlasting fire prepared for the devil and his angels! I was hungry and you gave me no food, I was thirsty and you gave me no drink. I was away from home and you gave me no welcome, naked and you gave me no clothing. I was ill and in prison and you did not come to comfort me'"* (*Matthew* 25:41-43 NAB).

Very clearly there is a connection between our works of charity and our eternal destiny. St. Paul confirms this:

> *For he will render to every man according to his works: to those who by patience in well-doing seek for glory and honor and immortality, he will give eternal*

*life; but for those who are factious and do not obey the
truth, but obey wickedness, there will be wrath and
fury (Romans 2:6-8).*

We quote a couple more Scriptures to make the point
absolutely clear:

*"An hour is coming in which all those in their tombs
shall hear his voice and come forth. Those who have
done right shall rise to live; the evildoers shall rise to
be damned" (John 5:28-29 NAB).*

*For we must all appear before the judgment seat of
Christ, so that each one may receive good or evil,
according to what he has done in the body (2
Corinthians 5:10).*

What then is the relationship between salvation, grace, faith,
and good works? What do the Scriptures say?

*For by grace you have been saved through faith; and
this is not your own doing, it is the gift of God—not
because of works, lest any man should boast. For we
are his workmanship, created in Christ Jesus for good
works, which God prepared beforehand, that we
should walk in them (Ephesians 2:8-10).*

Good works, then, are a fruit of genuine faith. If we have been
saved by Jesus by a free gift of mercy, we will desire to imitate
the works of Jesus out of gratitude and love. If we claim to have
faith, but there is no evidence in our actions, this may be "faith"
in name only:

*What does it profit, my brethren, if a man says he has
faith but has not works? Can his faith save him? . . .
Show me your faith apart from your works, and I by
my works will show you my faith. . . . For as the body
apart from the spirit is dead, so faith apart from works
is dead (James 2:14, 18, 26).*

Intercession

Full of joy and thanksgiving at our own salvation, we are eager to share this undeserved gift with others. One of the most powerful ways to help another person accept the Gospel is to pray for them.

> *Anyone who sees his brother sinning, if the sin is not deadly, should petition God, and thus life will be given to the sinner (1 John 5:16 NAB).*

St. Paul urges that

> *petitions, prayers, intercessions, and thanksgiving be offered for all men. . . . Prayer of this kind is good, and God our savior is pleased with it, for he wants all men to be saved and come to know the truth (1 Timothy 2:1, 3-4 NAB).*

Although it does not directly state so, this passage implies that our prayers help gain the salvation of others. Another Scripture on the power of prayer is found embedded in a passage on forgiving wrongs:

> *"If two of you agree on earth about anything they ask, it will be done for them by my Father in heaven" (Matthew 18:19).*

The context implies that joint prayer can bring about reconciliation between brothers. And there is no salvation without reconciliation because

> *"If you do not forgive men their trespasses, neither will your Father in heaven forgive your trespasses" (Matthew 6:15).*

St. Paul exhorts us to *"help carry one another's burdens; in that way you will fulfill the law of Christ"* (Galatians 6:2 NAB). Apparently he himself is doing so on behalf of the Galatians, since he writes,

You are my children, and you put me back in labor pains
until Christ is formed in you (Galatians 4:19 NAB).

The Scriptures capture several astonishing prayers of St. Paul
for his spiritual children (see *Ephesians* 3:14-21 and *Colossians*
1:9-12, for example).

Paul also says, writing of his Hebrew brothers and sisters,
"Brethren, my heart's desire and prayer to God for them is that
they may be saved" (Romans 10:1).

St. James teaches us that by laboring to restore sinners to
God's friendship, we benefit both the one we bring back from sin
and ourselves:

> *My brothers, the case may arise among you of some-*
> *one straying from the truth, and of another bringing*
> *him back. Remember this: the person who brings a*
> *sinner back from his way will save his soul from death*
> *and cancel a multitude of sins (James 5:19-20 NAB).*

Jesus Himself sets the prime example in this ministry of saving
intercession for

> *he is always able to save those who approach God*
> *through him, since he forever lives to make interces-*
> *sion for them (Hebrews 7:25 NAB).*

Witness to the Gospel

If we have received a word of truth that is able to save lives,
but do not share that word, have we really received that word
ourselves? Is it possible for there to be a fire in our hearts, but
one which sheds no light and brings no warmth to others?

> *The truthful witness saves lives, but he who utters lies*
> *is a betrayer (Proverbs 14:25 NAB).*

> *I have not hid thy saving help within my heart, I have*
> *spoken of thy faithfulness and thy salvation; I have not*
> *concealed thy steadfast love and thy faithfulness from*
> *the great congregation (Psalm 40:10).*

Jesus Himself was the original bearer of the good news in its fullness. To those who wanted Him to remain in their village he said, " *'To other towns I must announce the good news of the reign of God, because that is why I was sent'* " (*Luke* 4:43 NAB).

He in turn sent his disciples:

> *"Go into the whole world and proclaim the good news to all creation"* (*Mark* 16:15 NAB).

> *"You will receive power when the Holy Spirit comes down on you; then you are to be my witnesses in Jerusalem, throughout Judea and Samaria, yes, even to the ends of the earth"* (*Acts* 1:8 NAB).

When the Holy Spirit seizes a person and sets his heart on fire, he experiences a great impulse, a great urgency to express God's good news:

> *Necessity is laid upon me. Woe to me if I do not preach the gospel!* (*1 Corinthians* 9:16).

> *If I say, "I will not mention him, or speak any more in his name," there is in my heart as it were a burning fire shut up in my bones, and I am weary with holding it in, and I cannot* (*Jeremiah* 20:9).

St. John ignites our hearts as he tries to express the joy it brings him to tell us about Jesus:

> *That which was from the beginning, which we have heard, which we have seen with our eyes, which we have looked upon and touched with our hands, concerning the word of life—the life was made manifest, and we saw it, and testify to it, and proclaim to you the eternal life which was with the Father and was made manifest to us—that which we have seen and heard we proclaim also to you, so that you may have fellowship with us; and our fellowship is with the Father and with his Son Jesus Christ. And we are writing this that our joy may be complete* (*1 John* 1:1-4).

It is essential to the salvation of others that someone witness to
the Gospel:

> *But how are men to call upon him in whom they have*
> *not believed? And how are they to believe in him of*
> *whom they have never heard? And how are they to*
> *hear without a preacher? And how can men preach*
> *unless they are sent? (Romans 10:14-15).*

Some, after the pattern of the apostles, have a special mission
and special gifts to spend their lives preaching the word:

> *And the twelve summoned the body of the disciples*
> *and said, "It is not right that we should give up*
> *preaching the word of God to serve tables. . . . We will*
> *devote ourselves to prayer and to the ministry of the*
> *word" (Acts 6:2, 4).*

St. Paul, having been sent to preach the word of God by Jesus,
in his turn sends others. To Timothy he writes:

> *I charge you in the presence of God and of Jesus*
> *Christ who is to judge the living and the dead, and by*
> *his appearing and his kingdom: preach the word, be*
> *urgent in season and out of season, convince, rebuke,*
> *and exhort, be unfailing in patience and in teaching (2*
> *Timothy 4:1-2).*

But we all need to be a light in the darkness, joyfully spreading
the Gospel of Jesus through the fruit of holy lives, in both word
and deed:

> *"Nor do men light a lamp and put it under a bushel,*
> *but on a stand, and it gives light to all in the house.*
> *Let your light so shine before men, that they may see*
> *your good works and give glory to your Father who is*
> *in heaven" (Matthew 5:15-16).*

Does our faith lead us to speak up for Jesus?

> *Since we have the same spirit of faith as he had who*
> *wrote, "I believed, and so I spoke," we too believe,*

and so we speak (2 Corinthians 4:13).

"For we cannot but speak of what we have seen and heard" (Acts 4:20).

Jesus provides us with some powerful motivation to speak to others about Him:

"So every one who acknowledges me before men, I also will acknowledge before my Father who is in heaven; but whoever denies me before men, I also will deny before my Father who is in heaven" (Matthew 10:32-33).

A bonus reason to proclaim the Gospel to others, whether believers or unbelievers, is that preaching often inspires the preacher as much or more than the listeners. The same can be true with any other public expression of faith, such as public prayer before an abortion clinic, for instance. It would be just like God to try to convert us with words right out of our own mouths!

Forgiving Others

The following Scripture indicates that we cannot be saved if we do not extend to others the mercy and forgiveness we have received from our Father in Heaven:

"If you forgive men their trespasses, your heavenly Father also will forgive you; but if you do not forgive men their trespasses, neither will your Father forgive your trespasses" (Matthew 6:14-15).

Recall the parable Jesus told about the servant who, although he was forgiven a huge debt by the king, put in prison his fellow servant who owed him a trifle.

"His master sent for him and said, 'You worthless wretch! I canceled your entire debt when you pleaded with me. Should you not have dealt mercifully with your fellow servant, as I dealt with you?' Then in anger the master handed him over to the torturers until he paid back all that he owed. My heavenly

> *Father will treat you in exactly the same way unless each of you forgives his brother from his heart"* (*Matthew* 18:32-35 NAB).

Jesus exhorts us to have the merciful heart of His Father:

> *"Be merciful, even as your Father is merciful. Judge not, and you will not be judged; condemn not, and you will not be condemned; forgive, and you will be forgiven. . . . For the measure you give will be the measure you get back"* (*Luke* 6:36-37, 38).

Married and Single Life

Married life, when lived according to the Gospel of Jesus Christ, is a life laid down in generous love and service of others, first one's spouse and then one's children. There is plenty of opportunity to *"be subject to one another out of reverence for Christ"* (*Ephesians* 5:21) and plenty of opportunity to ask and extend forgiveness when we fail:

> *Let each one of you love his wife as himself, and let the wife see that she respects her husband. Children, obey your parents in the Lord, for this is right. "Honor your father and mother" (this is the first commandment with a promise), "that it may be well with you and that you may live long on the earth." Fathers, do not provoke your children to anger, but bring them up in the discipline and instruction of the Lord* (*Ephesians* 5:33-6:4).

> *You who are wives, be submissive to your husbands. This is your duty in the Lord. Husbands, love your wives. Avoid any bitterness toward them. You children, obey your parents in everything as the acceptable way in the Lord. And fathers, do not nag your children lest they lose heart* (*Colossians* 3:18-21 NAB).

The pattern for the joining of husband and wife as one flesh and the pattern for every family lies in the Holy Trinity:

God created man in his own image, in the image of
God he created him; male and female he created them.
And God blessed them, and God said to them, "Be
fruitful and multiply" (Genesis 1:27-28).

"From the beginning of creation, 'God made them
male and female.' 'For this reason a man shall leave
his father and mother and be joined to his wife, and
the two shall become one flesh.' So they are no longer
two but one flesh. What therefore God has joined
together, let no man put asunder" (Mark 10:6-9).

A Christian who is married to an unbeliever is able to bring
salvation to his or her spouse:

For the unbelieving husband is consecrated through
his wife, and the unbelieving wife is consecrated
through her husband. Otherwise, your children would
be unclean, but as it is they are holy (1 Corinthians
7:14).

Wife, how do you know that you will not save your
husband; or you, husband, that you will not save your
wife? (1 Corinthians 7:16 NAB).

This salvation is likely to be won more by example than by
words:

Likewise you wives, be submissive to your husbands,
so that some, though they do not obey the word, may
be won without a word by the behavior of their wives
(1 Peter 3:1).

Jesus has redeemed every aspect of human life, so that raising
a family while living a Christian life leads to salvation:

[The woman] will be saved through childbearing, pro-
vided she continues in faith and love and holiness—
her chastity being taken for granted (1 Timothy 2:15
NAB).

All fatherhood and motherhood, every family, is patterned after our Father in Heaven. St. Paul states, *"I kneel before the Father from whom every family in heaven and on earth takes its name"* (*Ephesians* 3:14-15 NAB). The family is the first school for the children and the parents are the first teachers:

> *"Take to heart these words which I enjoin on you today. Drill them into your children. Speak of them at home and abroad, whether you are busy or at rest. . . . Write them on the doorposts of your houses and on your gates"* (*Deuteronomy* 6:7, 9 NAB).

> *Hear, O sons, a father's instruction, and be attentive, that you may gain insight; for I give you good precepts; do not forsake my teaching. When I was a son with my father, tender, the only one in the sight of my mother, he taught me* (*Proverbs* 4:1-4).

We have an example, in the case of Timothy, of how faith in Jesus is likely to be passed on from generation to generation in families:

> *I am reminded of your sincere faith, a faith that dwelt first in your grandmother Lois and your mother Eunice and now, I am sure, dwells in you* (*2 Timothy* 1:5).

Children, too, must follow the example of Jesus, who obeyed Mary and Joseph: *"And he went down with them and came to Nazareth, and was obedient to them"* (*Luke* 2:51).

* * *

In Old Testament times it was considered to be a disgrace for a person to remain childless. We can see evidence of this in the story of John the Baptizer's mother, Elizabeth, who conceived miraculously in her old age:

> *Elizabeth conceived, and for five months she hid herself, saying, "Thus the Lord has done to me in the days when he looked on me, to take away my reproach among men"* (*Luke* 1:24-25).

*Now the time came for Elizabeth to be delivered, and
she gave birth to a son. And her neighbors and kins-
folk heard that the Lord had shown great mercy to her,
and they rejoiced with her (Luke 1:57-58).*

Elizabeth's childlessness was her "reproach among men" that
the Lord took away, showing her "great mercy." But even in the
Old Testament, there were a few indications that the LORD would
extend His favor to the unmarried and childless:

*[Let not] the eunuch say, "See, I am a dry tree." For
thus says the LORD: To the eunuchs who observe my
sabbaths and choose what pleases me and hold fast to
my covenant, I will give, in my house and within my
walls, a monument and a name better than sons and
daughters; an eternal, imperishable name will I give
them (Isaiah 56:3-5 NAB).*

In the New Testament, it is not a reproach to choose to be single for the sake of the Lord and His kingdom. Jesus Himself was
not married. St. Paul followed Jesus' example:

*Do we not have the right to marry a believing woman
like the rest of the apostles and the brothers of the
Lord and Cephas? (1 Corinthians 9:5 NAB).*

One glimpse Jesus gave us of resurrected life is a little surpris-
ing—no one will be married in Heaven:

*And Jesus said to them, "The sons of this age marry
and are given in marriage; but those who are
accounted worthy to attain to that age and to the resurrection from the dead neither marry nor are given in
marriage, for they cannot die any more, because they
are equal to angels and are sons of God, being sons of
the resurrection" (Luke 20:34-36).*

A person who chooses single life for the sake of the kingdom
can be a living witness to the life to come. Jesus encouraged
those who are capable of making this choice to make it:

> *"Not all men can receive this saying, but only those to whom it is given. . . . There are eunuchs who have made themselves eunuchs for the sake of the kingdom of heaven. He who is able to receive this, let him receive it"* (*Matthew* 19:11, 12).

St. Paul actually shows a preference for the single life. He argues that the duties of married life can be a distraction from single-hearted love of God:

> *I want you to be free from anxieties. The unmarried man is anxious about the affairs of the Lord, how to please the Lord; but the married man is anxious about worldly affairs, how to please his wife, and his interests are divided. And the unmarried woman or girl is anxious about the affairs of the Lord, how to be holy in body and spirit, but the married woman is anxious about worldly affairs, how to please her husband* (*1 Corinthians* 7:32-34).

* * *

For these reasons, the Catholic Church highly exalts both marriage and the family, and the calling to be single for the Lord.

Matrimony is one of the seven sacraments. The essence of the sacrament is the exchange of consent between a baptized man and a baptized woman who are free to marry. The bond which is thereby formed is sealed by God and cannot be broken (see *Mark* 10:9). In the sacrament, their human love is elevated to become like Christ's love for the Church (see *Ephesians* 5:21-32). This love tends toward a deep union of the spouses with each other and with Jesus. It must be open to bearing fruit in the co-creation (with God the Creator) of children, each one a new, unique person who will live forever. It is in the intimate love of the family home that the most basic and natural church community forms.

From the time of the apostles, virgins have heeded the call of Jesus to "those who can accept it" and have chosen Him alone as their spouse. When they live their call joyfully, they are a powerful sign of the kingdom. There is no sacrament for the choice of virginity that corresponds to the sacrament of Matrimony. But this call can be lived out in many ways from informal to very formal. A single lay person can secretly commit her life to Jesus; virgins can be consecrated to God by the diocesan bishop according to a liturgical rite; a person can enter religious life, professing vows of poverty, chastity, and obedience; and many other variations.

Since both Matrimony and virginity are from Jesus, they cannot in any way be in competition, but are both exalted ways of life, if they are truly lived for the Lord. Either can be a happy and fulfilling vocation for the person who is called accordingly.

Section 3

CHRISTIAN MATURITY

The Scriptures frequently compare Christian growth to natural growth. Baptism is like birth; we are urged to grow out of spiritual childhood; our goal is to arrive at full maturity in Christ. We have put into this section the conditions for salvation which can be fulfilled by one who has been sincerely living the Christian life for some time and making progress in holiness.

Suffering

We sometimes imagine that an ideal world would be one in which there is no suffering. But if it had been in our best interest to eliminate suffering, a loving and almighty God would certainly have done so as part of our salvation. Instead, the Father sent His only Son Jesus, His Beloved One, to enter our world as it is, suffering and all. He came to save us, not *from* our suffering, but *in* our suffering.

Jesus has promised to bring us abundant life (see *John* 10:10). If "life to the full" means to live vividly, fully alive, fully experiencing life, then it means great intensity in both our joys and our sufferings. The opposite of "life to the full" would be a timid and fearful life of depressing monotony, a living death.

Jesus Himself certainly lived life boldly and deeply, fully embracing whatever God sent His way, whether exultant joy, great grief, or bodily torture.

God is able to create tremendous good out of suffering if we allow Him. Jesus has given us the supreme example: by freely accepting His Passion and death at our hands (the greatest crime in human history), He won eternal salvation for us (the greatest good in human history):

> *Indeed, it was fitting that when bringing many sons to glory God, for whom and through whom all things exist, should make their leader in the work of salvation perfect through suffering* (Hebrews 2:10 NAB).

St. Paul, who exhorts us to follow his own example, exclaims:

> *Now I rejoice in my suffering for your sake, and in my flesh I complete what is lacking in Christ's afflictions for the sake of his body, that is, the church* (Colossians 1:24).

St. Peter shows the place of suffering in the life of the Christian and what our attitude should be toward it:

> *There is cause for rejoicing here. You may for a time have to suffer the distress of many trials; but this is so that your faith, which is more precious than the passing splendor of fire-tried gold, may by its genuineness lead to praise, glory, and honor when Jesus Christ appears . . . because you are achieving faith's goal, your salvation* (1 Peter 1:6-7, 9 NAB).

By accepting our suffering in the same way Jesus accepted His, God can transform us from being lost in our own self-centeredness to becoming fully awake to ourselves in self-giving generosity:

> *We even boast of our afflictions! We know that affliction makes for endurance, and endurance for tested virtue, and tested virtue for hope. And this hope will not leave us disappointed, because the love of God has been poured out in our hearts through the Holy Spirit who has been given to us* (Romans 5:3-5 NAB).

True love is always focused on the beloved; we will do anything for the good of the ones we love:

> *If we are afflicted, it is for your comfort and salvation; and if we are comforted, it is for your comfort, which you experience when you patiently endure the same sufferings that we suffer* (2 Corinthians 1:6).

> *Therefore I endure everything for the sake of the elect,*
> *that they also may obtain salvation in Christ Jesus*
> *with its eternal glory (2 Timothy 2:10).*

Anyone who follows Jesus' path to eternal life can expect to suffer:

> *[Paul and Barnabas] gave their disciples reassur-*
> *ances, and encouraged them to persevere in the faith*
> *with this instruction: "We must undergo many trials if*
> *we are to enter into the reign of God" (Acts 14:22*
> *NAB).*

> *Indeed all who desire to live a godly life in Christ*
> *Jesus will be persecuted (2 Timothy 3:12).*

The suffering which is most like Jesus' suffering is the persecution which comes with proclaiming the Gospel:

> *"Blest are those persecuted for holiness' sake; the*
> *reign of God is theirs. Blest are you when they insult*
> *you and persecute you and utter every kind of slander*
> *against you because of me. Be glad and rejoice, for*
> *your reward is great in heaven; they persecuted the*
> *prophets before you in the very same way" (Matthew*
> *5:10-12 NAB).*

In comparison with the joy and the glory that is to come, any suffering we endure in this life is a small thing:

> *This slight momentary affliction is preparing for us an*
> *eternal weight of glory beyond all comparison (2*
> *Corinthians 4:17).*

> *[Let us look to Jesus], who for the joy that was set*
> *before him endured the cross, despising the shame,*
> *and is seated at the right hand of the throne of God*
> *(Hebrews 12:2).*

> *Happy the man who holds out to the end through trial!*
> *Once he has been proved, he will receive the crown of*
> *life the Lord has promised to those who love him*
> *(James 1:12 NAB).*

Dying to Self

The tell-tale sign of genuine love is a generous outpouring of self for others. Our attitude must be that of Christ, who

> *though he was in the form of God, he did not deem equality with God something to be grasped at. Rather, he emptied himself* (*Philippians* 2:6-7 NAB).

If we find that we are grabbing or clutching for anyone or anything other than Jesus, it is a good sign that our love is not fully genuine. Jesus said, " *'Whoever loves father or mother, son or daughter, more than me is not worthy of me'* " (*Matthew* 10:37 NAB). It is good for our spiritual health to release any hold we may have on others:

> *"There is no one who has left house or brothers or sisters or mother or father or children or lands, for my sake and the gospel, who will not receive a hundredfold now in this time, houses and brothers and sisters and mothers and children and lands, with persecutions, and in the age to come eternal life"* (*Mark* 10:29-30).

Jesus said, " *'He who loves his life loses it, and he who hates his life in this world will keep it for eternal life'* " (*John* 12:25). And again, " *'If any man would come after me, let him deny himself and take up his cross daily and follow me'* " (*Luke* 9:23).

St. Paul indicates that this denial of self is not merely a mental thing, when he says,

> *I do not run like a man who loses sight of the finish line. I do not fight as if I were shadowboxing. What I do is discipline my own body and master it, for fear that after having preached to others I myself should be rejected* (*1 Corinthians* 9:26-27 NAB).

We do not desire to die to self merely for our own benefit, but primarily to better love and serve others. Again, St. Paul says:

> *Though I am free from all men, I have made myself a slave to all, that I might win the more. . . . To the weak*

I became weak, that I might win the weak. I have become all things to all men, that I might by all means save some (1 Corinthians 9:19, 22).

I try to please all men in everything I do, not seeking my own advantage, but that of the many, that they may be saved (1 Corinthians 10:33).

Another beneficial way to die to self is to accept correction from the Lord when it comes:

Do not withhold discipline from a child; if you beat him with a rod, he will not die. If you beat him with a rod you will save his life from Sheol (Proverbs 23:13-14).

The discipline of the LORD, my son, disdain not; spurn not his reproof; for whom the LORD loves he reproves, and he chastises the son he favors (Proverbs 3:11-12 NAB).

God is treating you as sons; for what son is there whom his father does not discipline? If you are left without discipline, in which you have all participated, then you are illegitimate children and not sons. Besides this, we have had earthly fathers to discipline us and we respected them. Shall we not much more be subject to the Father of spirits and live? For they disciplined us for a short time at their pleasure, but he disciplines us for our good, that we may share his holiness. For the moment all discipline seems painful rather than pleasant; later it yields the peaceful fruit of righteousness to those who have been trained by it (Hebrews 12:7-11).

God's ways are not our ways. Unless it had been revealed in God's word, who would have guessed that dying to oneself is also a way to offer genuine worship to our Father?

I appeal to you therefore, brethren, by the mercies of God, to present your bodies as a living sacrifice, holy and acceptable to God, which is your spiritual worship (Romans 12:1).

Humility

True humility always accompanies a real encounter with the LORD. We are awed by His presence, bow down to worship Him, and are ready to obey Him in everything. We have, perhaps for the first time in our lives, a realistic concept of our own stature before God. This first taste of genuine humility is in danger of fading away, however. A man becomes truly humble only when his whole way of life over a long time is permeated by fear of the LORD:

> *This is the one whom I approve: the lowly and afflicted man who trembles at my word (Isaiah 66:2 NAB).*

Jesus, in the parable of the Pharisee and the tax collector, helps us to see what true humility is. The Pharisee was the opposite of humble—he was one of those *"who trusted in themselves that they were righteous and despised others"* (*Luke* 18:9). The Scripture passage goes on:

> *"The [tax collector], however, kept his distance, not even daring to raise his eyes to heaven. All he did was beat his breast and say, 'O God, be merciful to me, a sinner.' Believe me, this man went home from the temple justified but the other did not. For everyone who exalts himself shall be humbled while he who humbles himself shall be exalted"* (*Luke* 18:13-14 NAB).

There is a natural connection between humility and willingness to serve others. Jesus said,

> *"Whoever would be great among you must be your servant, and whoever would be first among you must be your slave; even as the Son of man came not to be served but to serve, and to give his life as a ransom for many"* (*Matthew* 20:26-28).

After washing the feet of His disciples, a task ordinarily done by a slave, Jesus said, *" 'Do you know what I have done to you? You call me Teacher and Lord; and you are right, for so I am. If I then, your Lord and Teacher, have washed your feet, you also ought to wash one another's feet' "* (*John* 13:12-14).

When our fundamental outlook is concern for the benefit of others rather than for our own benefit, we are becoming truly humble:

> *Do nothing from selfishness or conceit, but in humility count others better than yourselves. Let each of you look not only to his own interests, but also to the interests of others. Have this mind among yourselves, which is yours in Christ Jesus, who . . . being found in human form he humbled himself* (*Philippians* 2:3-5, 8).

The one who has nothing and who knows he *is* nothing is one Jesus can bring to salvation:

> *The LORD is near to the brokenhearted, and saves the crushed in spirit* (*Psalm* 34:18).

> *For he delivers the needy when he calls, the poor and him who has no helper. He has pity on the weak and the needy, and saves the lives of the needy* (*Psalm* 72:12-13).

> *The LORD keeps the little ones; I was brought low, and he saved me* (*Psalm* 116:6 NAB).

> *For God abases the proud, but he saves the lowly* (*Job* 22:29).

Jesus loves the little children so much because they depend so trustingly on others for everything:

> *"Whoever humbles himself like this child, he is the greatest in the kingdom of heaven"* (*Matthew* 18:4).

> *"Truly, I say to you, whoever does not receive the kingdom of God like a child shall not enter it"* (*Mark* 10:15).

Poverty

It is hard to ignore what Jesus said about poverty for the sake of the kingdom. It is also difficult to explain away Jesus' sayings on poverty as merely allegorical:

> *"Blessed are you poor, for yours is the kingdom of God" (Luke 6:20).*

> *Jesus looked around and said to his disciples, "How hard it will be for those who have riches to enter the kingdom of God!" (Mark 10:23).*

> *"Avoid greed in all its forms. A man may be wealthy, but his possessions do not guarantee him life" (Luke 12:15 NAB).*

It is not poverty for the sake of being poor that Jesus speaks of. It is poverty for the sake of His kingdom.

> *"The kingdom of heaven is like treasure hidden in a field, which a man found and covered up; then in his joy he goes and sells all that he has and buys that field" (Matthew 13:44).*

> *"Or again, the kingdom of heaven is like a merchant's search for fine pearls. When he found one really valuable pearl, he went back and put up for sale all that he had and bought it" (Matthew 13:45-46 NAB).*

In the end, poverty for the sake of the kingdom is always chosen because it leads to a greater good. As St. Paul says of Jesus,

> *He was rich, yet for your sake he became poor, so that by his poverty you might become rich (2 Corinthians 8:9).*

To the rich young man, Jesus advised:

> *"If you seek perfection, go, sell your possessions, and give to the poor. You will then have treasure in heaven. Afterward, come back and follow me" (Matthew 19:21 NAB).*

There seems to be a relationship between material poverty and spiritual wealth: *"Has not God chosen those who are poor in the world to be rich in faith and heirs of the kingdom?" (James 2:5).* Indeed, the opposite is also true: too many possessions can crowd out what is important in life:

And Lot, who went with Abram, also had flocks and herds and tents, so that the land could not support both of them dwelling together, for their possessions were so great that they could not dwell together (Genesis 13:5-6).

Guard Our Speech

Our salvation depends on what we say and how we say it. Sooner or later whatever fills our heart and our thoughts will get out; we cannot help but express what is inside us through our words, our attitude, our tone of voice, our body language, and our actions:

"A good man produces goodness from the good in his heart; an evil man produces evil out of his store of evil. Each man speaks from his heart's abundance" (Luke 6:45 NAB).

A baby Christian is very likely to be *"still of the flesh"* (*1 Corinthians* 3:3). Since whatever fills the heart flows out of the mouth, a spiritual infant probably will not consistently bring forth goodness in speech. The Scriptures indicate that the tongue is the last member of our body to come under our control:

All of us fall short in many respects. If a person is without fault in speech he is a man in the fullest sense, because he can control his entire body. . . . We use [the tongue] to say, "Praised be the Lord and Father"; then we use it to curse men, though they are made in the likeness of God. Blessing and curse come out of the same mouth. This ought not to be, my brothers! (James 3:2, 9-10 NAB).

Besides revealing the abundance of our heart, the words which come out of our mouth have an effect on other people—an effect for good or for evil:

A gentle tongue is a tree of life, but perverseness in it breaks the spirit (Proverbs 15:4).

*A fountain of life is the mouth of the just, but the
mouth of the wicked conceals violence (Proverbs
10:11 NAB).*

Because of the power of the tongue to urge others to either
good or evil, St. Paul exhorts us: *"Let no evil talk come out of
your mouths, but only such as is good for edifying, as fits the
occasion, that it may impart grace to those who
hear"* (*Ephesians* 4:29).

In addition to the good or evil that comes to others through
what we say, we ourselves gain or lose depending on our words:

*He who guards his mouth protects his life; to open
wide one's lips bring downfall (Proverbs 13:3 NAB).*

*Death and life are in the power of the tongue; those
who make it a friend shall eat its fruit (Proverbs 18:21
NAB).*

*"He that would love life and see good days, let him
keep his tongue from evil and his lips from speaking
guile" (1 Peter 3:10).*

Jesus confirms that, indeed, our salvation hinges on our
speech:

*"I tell you, on the day of judgment men will render
account for every careless word they utter; for by your
words you will be justified, and by your words you will
be condemned" (Matthew 12:36-37).*

Wait for the Lord

When things are not going the way we like, we are apt to take
matters into our own hands. It seems to be better to do something—*anything*—than to turn to God and allow Him to take
charge. But sometimes we get stuck in impossible-seeming situa-
tions.

When the Israelites were trapped, in a panic, between
Pharaoh's army on the one side and the Red Sea on the other,

Moses said to the people,

> *"Fear not! Stand your ground, and you will see the*
> *victory the LORD will win for you today. . . . The LORD*
> *himself will fight for you; you have only to keep still"*
> (*Exodus* 14:13-14 NAB).

Waiting on the LORD implies trusting Him even though it doesn't look like anything is happening.

> *For thus said the Lord GOD, The Holy One of Israel,*
> *"In returning and rest you shall be saved; in quietness*
> *and in trust shall be your strength" (Isaiah* 30:15*).*

This quiet trust is the fruit of life-long prayer:

> *I have calmed and quieted my soul, like a child qui-*
> *eted at its mother's breast; like a child that is quieted*
> *is my soul (Psalm* 131:2).

> *For God alone my soul waits in silence; from him comes*
> *my salvation. He only is my rock and my salvation, my*
> *fortress; I shall not be greatly moved (Psalm* 62:1-2).

Those who wait on the Lord instead of rushing ahead on their own strength find that they have energy enough for the long haul:

> *They that hope in the LORD will renew their strength,*
> *they will soar as with eagles' wings; they will run and*
> *not grow weary, walk and not grow faint (Isaiah* 40:31
> NAB).

Scoffers and mockers demand to see immediate action:

> *Scoffers will come in the last days with scoffing, fol-*
> *lowing their own passions and saying "Where is the*
> *promise of his coming? For ever since the fathers fell*
> *asleep, all things have continued as they were from the*
> *beginning of creation" (2 Peter* 3:3-4).

> *So also the chief priests mocked [Jesus] to one*
> *another with the scribes, saying, "He saved others; he*

cannot save himself. Let the Christ, the King of Israel, come down from the cross, that we may see and believe" (*Mark* 15:31-32).

But the Lord, speaking through the prophet Isaiah, has stern words for those who demand an account from God:

Woe to those . . . who say: "Let him make haste, let him speed his work that we may see it; let the purpose of the Holy One of Israel draw near, and let it come, that we may know it!" (*Isaiah* 5:18-19).

What seems to us to be a delay is really a work of mercy by God—He is holding open the door of salvation a little longer so as many as possible may be saved:

The Lord does not delay in keeping his promise— though some consider it "delay." Rather, he shows you generous patience, since he wants none to perish but all to come to repentance (*2 Peter* 3:9 NAB).

What a marvelous God we have! But how far our hearts are from His. His is full of mercy, while ours are full of impatience. May we learn to be more like Jesus:

But as for me, I will look to the LORD, I will wait for the God of my salvation; my God will hear me (*Micah* 7:7).

The LORD is good to those who wait for him, to the soul that seeks him. It is good that one should wait quietly for the salvation of the LORD (*Lamentations* 3:25-26).

Hope in the Lord

Hope involves looking forward to something good that has not come yet. Hope has to do with waiting eagerly for a promise to be fulfilled:

Hope is not hope if its object is seen; how is it possible for one to hope for what he sees? And hoping for what we cannot see means awaiting it with patient endurance (*Romans* 8:24-25 NAB).

Our hope can be in things good or bad. We can look ahead to self-gratification or to self-giving. Each bears its own reward as stated in *Proverbs* 10:28: "*The hope of the just brings them joy, but the expectation of the wicked comes to nought.*"

The hopeful Christian waits on the Lord:

> *Our hopes are fixed on the living God who is the savior of all men, but especially of those who believe* (*1 Timothy* 4:10 NAB).

The Christian waits on the Lord in joyful hope. "*We rejoice in our hope of sharing the glory of God*" (*Romans* 5:2).

It is necessary for us to have Christian hope to be saved? St. Paul is clear: "*In hope we were saved*" (*Romans* 8:24 NAB). This is because we do not yet possess eternal life in its fullness:

> *[We have been] sealed with the Holy Spirit who had been promised. He is the pledge of our inheritance, the first payment against the full redemption of a people God has made his own, to praise his glory* (*Ephesians* 1:13-14 NAB).

Indeed, we are "*heirs in hope of eternal life*" (*Titus* 3:7), that is, we do not yet taste it, but by hope we possess it now. It is good to hope for salvation, "*the free gift of God . . . eternal life in Christ Jesus our Lord*" (*Romans* 6:23).

> *I hope for thy salvation, O LORD, and I do thy commandments* (*Psalm* 119:166).

Our hope is not for our own salvation only, but for the salvation of all God's people. And, if our hope is in God, our hope is in a sure thing:

> *This hope will not leave us disappointed, because the love of God has been poured out in our hearts through the Holy Spirit who has been given to us* (*Romans* 5:5 NAB).

Only in God be at rest, my soul, for from him comes my hope. He only is my rock and my salvation, my stronghold; I shall not be disturbed (Psalm 62:6-7 NAB).

The author of the *Letter to the Hebrews* goes to great lengths to describe how certain God's promise is:

When God desired to show more convincingly to the heirs of the promise the unchangeable character of his purpose, he interposed with an oath, so that through two unchangeable things, in which it is impossible that God should prove false, we . . . [might] seize the hope set before us (Hebrews 6:17-18).

St. Paul also underlines God's trustworthiness when he greets Titus *"in hope of eternal life which God, who never lies, promised ages ago" (Titus 1:1).* God's promise is so solid that He desires us to

seize the hope set before us. We have this as a sure and steadfast anchor of the soul, a hope that enters into the inner shrine behind the curtain, where Jesus has gone as a forerunner on our behalf (Hebrews 6:18-20).

Hope of future glory can sustain us when life gets tough:

This I call to mind, and therefore I have hope: The steadfast love of the LORD never ceases, his mercies never come to an end; they are new every morning; great is thy faithfulness. "The LORD is my portion," says my soul, "therefore I will hope in him" (Lamentations 3:21-24).

But see, the eyes of the LORD are upon those who fear him, upon those who hope for his kindness, to deliver them from death and preserve them in spite of famine (Psalm 33:18-19 NAB).

The hope of salvation is part of the armor of God, protecting us from losing heart in a world filled with darkness:

*Since we belong to the day, let us be sober, and put on
the breastplate of faith and love, and for a helmet the
hope of salvation (1 Thessalonians 5:8).*

As a fitting closing, we echo St. Paul's prayer for you:

*May the God of hope fill you with all joy and peace in
believing, so that by the power of the Holy Spirit you
may abound in hope (Romans 15:13).*

Perseverance

There are some who believe that salvation, once obtained, cannot be lost. But a wider look at what the Scriptures say does not support this view. The Scriptures repeatedly exhort us to persevere, to "hang in there." It is only the one who endures to the end who will be saved.

There are several Scriptures that make it clear that it is possible for a believer to apostasize, that is, totally reject his faith:

*For when men have once been enlightened and have
tasted the heavenly gift and become sharers in the
Holy Spirit, when they have tasted the good word of
God and the powers of the age to come, and then have
fallen away, it is impossible to make them repent
again, since they are crucifying the Son of God for
themselves and holding him up to contempt (Hebrews
6:4-6 NAB).*

St. Peter warns us to take steps to avoid a fall, making it plain that a fall is possible:

*Therefore, brethren, be the more zealous to confirm
your call and election, for if you do this you will never
fall; so there will be richly provided for you an
entrance into the eternal kingdom of our Lord and
Savior Jesus Christ (2 Peter 1:10-11).*

None of us is to take it for granted that we are in good standing with God:

Take care, brethren, lest there be in any of you an evil, unbelieving heart, leading you to fall away from the living God. . . . For we share in Christ, if only we hold our first confidence firm to the end (Hebrews 3:12, 14).

Consider the kindness and the severity of God—severity toward those who fell, kindness toward you, provided you remain in his kindness; if you do not, you too will be cut off (Romans 11:22 NAB).

Even the great St. Paul does not talk as if he has a guarantee of salvation. On the contrary, he tells us, *"I do not run like a man who loses sight of the finish line. I do not fight as if I were shadowboxing. What I do is discipline my own body and master it, for fear that after having preached to others I myself should be rejected"* (*1 Corinthians* 9:26-27 NAB).

Speaking of the end times, Jesus said,

"They will deliver you up to tribulation, and put you to death; and you will be hated by all nations for my name's sake. And then many will fall away, and betray one another, and hate one another. And many false prophets will arise and lead men astray. And because wickedness is multiplied, most men's love will grow cold. But he who endures to the end will be saved" (*Matthew* 24:9-13).

Perseverance is related to zeal. Our natural tendency is to find our energies dwindle and our resolve dissolve. Without the supernatural pilot light of the Holy Spirit we will burn out:

Our desire is that each of you show the same zeal to the end, fully assured of that for which you hope. Do not grow lazy, but imitate those who, through faith and patience, are inheriting the promises (Hebrews 6:11-12 NAB).

There is a defensive quality to perseverance; no matter how the enemy surges at us, we will dig in and resist at all costs, using the armor God has given us:

Finally, draw your strength from the Lord and his mighty power. Put on the armor of God so that you may be able to stand firm against the tactics of the devil (Ephesians 6:10-11 NAB).

In addition there is "offensive" perseverance, where we go on the attack wielding *"the weapons of righteousness for the right hand and for the left"* (*2 Corinthians* 6:7). Indeed *"the weapons of our warfare are not worldly but have divine power to destroy strongholds"* (*2 Corinthians* 10:4). The kingdom of darkness is no match for our labor of love:

Therefore, my beloved brethren, be steadfast, immovable, always abounding in the work of the Lord, knowing that in the Lord your labor is not in vain (1 Corinthians 15:58).

Jesus warns us to be on the watch; we must be prepared at all times for His return! This means we must persevere in faith, hope, and love over the long haul, living each day in readiness for judgment:

"The groom arrived, and the ones who were ready went into the wedding with him. Then the door was barred. Later the other bridesmaids came back. 'Master, master!' they cried. 'Open the door for us.' But he answered, 'I tell you, I do not know you.' The moral is: keep your eyes open, for you know not the day or the hour" (Matthew 25:10-13 NAB).

We endure trials, not alone, but as part of the community of faith. The generous efforts of one member of the Body of Christ can help obtain the salvation of others:

Therefore I endure everything for the sake of the elect, that they also may obtain salvation in Christ Jesus with its eternal glory (2 Timothy 2:10).

At last, after a lifetime of persevering in the faith in the face of all odds, by God's grace we enter into our reward:

Blessed is the man who endures trial, for when he has

stood the test he will receive the crown of life which
God has promised to those who love him (*James* 1:12).

"*Be faithful unto death, and I will give you the crown
of life*" (*Revelation* 2:10).

Maturity

Every living creature in the natural world that does not grow
and develop dies. It is no different with our spiritual life. And so
the Scriptures urge us to grow to spiritual maturity. In fact, it is
essential to salvation to grow up spiritually:

> *Like newborn babes, long for pure spiritual milk, that
> by it you may grow up to salvation* (*1 Peter* 2:2).

To remain spiritually immature through one's own fault is an
obstacle to salvation:

> *There is, to be sure, a certain wisdom which we
> express among the spiritually mature. . . . Brothers,
> the trouble was that I could not talk to you as spiritual
> men but only as men of flesh, as infants in Christ. I fed
> you with milk, and did not give you solid food because
> you were not ready for it. You are not ready for it even
> now, being still very much in a natural condition* (*1
> Corinthians* 2:6, 3:1-3 NAB).

> *Those who are in the flesh cannot please God*
> (*Romans* 8:8).

> *Therefore let us leave the elementary doctrine of
> Christ and go on to maturity* (*Hebrews* 6:1).

If we are going to remain like children in anything, says St.
Paul, let it be in childlike innocence from sin:

> *Brothers, do not be childish in your outlook. Be like
> children as far as evil is concerned, but in mind be
> mature* (*1 Corinthians* 14:20 NAB).

A mark of physical maturity is the ability to reproduce one's own kind. It is clear from the Scriptures that the Father wants us to produce good fruit in abundance:

> *"By this my Father is glorified, that you bear much fruit, and so prove to be my disciples"* (*John* 15:8).

> *"He who abides in me, and I in him, he it is that bears much fruit, for apart from me you can do nothing"* (*John* 15:5).

> *"It was not you who chose me, it was I who chose you to go forth and bear fruit. Your fruit must endure"* (*John* 15:16 NAB).

Only those who take Jesus' word into a good and honest heart can bear fruit in abundance. There are also unfruitful ways to receive the Gospel message:

> *"This is the meaning of the parable. The seed is the word of God. Those on the footpath are people who hear, but the devil comes and takes the word out of their hearts lest they believe and be saved. Those on the rocky ground are the ones who, when they hear the word, receive it with joy. They have no root; they believe for a while, but fall away in time of temptation. The seed fallen among briars are those who hear, but their progress is stifled by the cares and riches and pleasures of life and they do not mature. The seed on good ground are those who hear the word in a spirit of openness, retain it, and bear fruit through persever-ance"* (*Luke* 8:11-15 NAB).

It is vital to "hold fast to the word," not falling away when other, more attractive "gospels" come along, if we are to produce good fruit for the kingdom.

Not only individual Christians, but the whole Body of Christ grows to maturity:

> *[Hold fast to the Head], from whom the whole body, nourished and knit together through its joints and lig-*

aments, grows with a growth that is from God (Colossians 2:19).

[When Jesus ascended on high, he gave gifts to men] to build up the body of Christ, till we become one in faith and in the knowledge of God's Son, and form that perfect man who is Christ come to full stature. Let us, then, be children no longer, tossed here and there, carried about by every wind of doctrine that originates in human trickery and skill in proposing error. Rather, let us profess the truth in love and grow to the full maturity of Christ the head. Through him the whole body grows, and with the proper functioning of the members joined firmly together by each supporting ligament, builds itself up in love (Ephesians 4:12-16 NAB).

Some elements of spiritual maturity are mentioned in the quote above: speaking the truth in love; attaining to the unity of the faith; attaining to the knowledge of the Son of God; no longer being tossed to and fro by evil.

No matter what stage of growth we are at (or think we are at), those who love Jesus will aim for more. St. Paul, aware that not to go forward is go backward, implores us:

Finally, brethren, we beseech and exhort you in the Lord Jesus, that as you learned from us how you ought to live and to please God, just as you are doing, you do so more and more. . . . Indeed you do love all the brethren throughout Macedonia. But we exhort you, brethren, to do so more and more (1 Thessalonians 4:1, 10).

The miracle of spiritual growth, just like natural growth, comes from God. The farmer can help the process by preparing the ground and sowing the seed, but after that he can only wait and pray for good weather while the mystery of growth takes place beyond his control:

I planted, Apollos watered, but God gave the growth. So neither he who plants nor he who waters is anything, but only God who gives the growth (1 Corinthians 3:6-7).

"This is how it is with the reign of God. A man scatters seed on the ground. He goes to bed and gets up day after day. Through it all the seed sprouts and grows without his knowing how it happens. The soil produces of itself first the blade, then the ear, finally the ripe wheat in the ear. When the crop is ready he 'wields the sickle, for the time is ripe for harvest'" (*Mark* 4:26-29 NAB).

Jesus tells a parable which hints that the opposition of evil can help a Christian come to full maturity:

"The kingdom of heaven may be compared to a man who sowed good seed in his field; but while men were sleeping, his enemy came and sowed weeds among the wheat, and went away. So when the plants came up and bore grain, then the weeds appeared also. And the servants of the householder came and said to him, 'Sir, did you not sow good seed in your field? How then has it weeds?' He said to them, 'An enemy has done this.' The servants said to him, 'Then do you want us to go and gather them?' But he said, 'No; lest in gathering the weeds you root up the wheat along with them. Let both grow together until the harvest; and at harvest time I will tell the reapers, gather the weeds first and bind them in bundles to be burned, but gather the wheat into my barn'" (*Matthew* 13:24-30).

It is better for the "sons of the kingdom" to come to full maturity even if they have to live in close quarters with the "sons of the evil one" than it is to risk accidentally uprooting them before they come to full maturity. In fact, learning how to love those who persecute us is to grow in Christian maturity.

There may be another lesson to learn from this parable. A species of weed grows in Palestine that is almost impossible to distinguish from the wheat until they are both mature—and then it is too late to pull up the weeds because the roots of both are so intertwined (Barclay, *The Gospel of Matthew,* Volume 2, pp. 72-73). Perhaps with people, too, it is difficult to distinguish the good from the bad till we have grown to full maturity.

Growing in Love

What is love? The word is used so many ways in the English language it is sometimes hard to know what is meant by it.

When we look at the cross of Jesus, we see true love revealed. We see that His kind of love involves the total outpouring of oneself for the good of the beloved. This love involves a great generosity, to the point of an emptying of self, to the point of death of self, anything, for the benefit of the beloved.

Love is directly opposed to any sort of grabbing or clutching or draining from others. Sin tends to seize control, to have its own way, especially at the expense of the weak. Love loves to yield itself to the other, to spend itself for the beloved. Every sin, then, is a sin against the law of love:

> *The commandments . . . are all summed up in this, "You shall love your neighbor as yourself." Love never wrongs the neighbor, hence love is the fulfillment of the law (Romans 13:9, 10 NAB).*

God's desire is to form us into lovers after the likeness of Jesus. By the power of the Holy Spirit, we can be transformed into agents of reconciliation and divine love in the world, bringing God's mercy to those who so desperately need it.

Love is the culmination of the Gospel. Delivered from sin by God Who is love, we are free to love as He loves. If we are attached to Jesus, the Vine (see *John* 15:5), we have His divine life, His power to love, flowing through us: *"God is love, and he who abides in love abides in God, and God in him"* (*1 John* 4:16 NAB).

Can one who does not love be saved?

> *"Eternal life is this: to know you, the only true God,*

and him whom you have sent, Jesus Christ" (John 17:3 NAB);

but

The man without love has known nothing of God, for God is love (1 John 4:8 NAB).

St. John is even more plain in the following quote:

He who does not love abides in death. Any one who hates his brother is a murderer, and you know that no murderer has eternal life abiding in him (1 John 3:14-15).

To love as Jesus loves means more than talking about it: *"Little children, let us not love in word or speech but in deed and in truth" (1 John 3:18).*

To erase all doubts, Jesus made the good news of love into a command:

"This is my commandment, that you love one another as I have loved you. Greater love has no man than this, that a man lay down his life for his friends. You are my friends if you do what I command you" (John 15:12-14).

The one who loves in truth loves his enemies. This kind of love can free the enemy to eventually respond in love. If we do this, we are following the pattern of and multiplying Jesus' freeing, redemptive love: *"We, for our part, love because he first loved us" (1 John 4:19 NAB).* As sons of the Father, we are loving as He is loving:

"Do to others what you would have them do to you. If you love those who love you, what credit is that to you? Even sinners love those who love them. . . . Love your enemy and do good; lend without expecting repayment. Then will your recompense be great. You will rightly be called sons of the Most High, since he himself is good to the ungrateful and the wicked" (Luke 6:31-32, 35 NAB).

In his great passage on love, St. Paul illustrates the pre-eminence of love:

> *If I have faith great enough to move mountains, but have not love, I am nothing. If I give everything I have to feed the poor and hand over my body to be burned, but have not love, I gain nothing (1 Corinthians* 13:2-3 NAB).

Love, growing ever stronger, triumphs into all eternity:

> *[For] love never ends. . . . Faith, hope, love abide, these three; but the greatest of these is love (1 Corinthians* 13:8, 13).

In the end, love overwhelms sin and evil: *"Love covers a multitude of sins"* (*1 Peter* 4:8). Even death is no match for love. *"Love is strong as death" (Song of Songs* 8:6*).*

> *"Death is swallowed up in victory." "O death, where is your victory? O death, where is your sting?" (1 Corinthians* 15:54-55 NAB).

God has given a beautiful promise to those who love Him:

> *Because he cleaves to me in love, I will deliver him; I will protect him, because he knows my name. When he calls to me, I will answer him; I will be with him in trouble, I will rescue him and honor him. With long life I will satisfy him, and show him my salvation (Psalm* 91:14-16).

Section 4

COMMUNITY IN THE CHURCH

Behold, how good and pleasant it is when brothers dwell in unity! (Psalm 133:1).

The context of salvation is communal. St. Jude refers to this in passing: *"Beloved, being very eager to write to you of our common salvation . . ." (Jude 3).* Although the experience of conversion to Christ is an intensely personal one, it does not come about in isolation, but in the company of others who also have turned their backs on the world and embraced Jesus. Indeed, before we are able to make a decision to give our lives to the Lord, we must have heard of Him:

How can they believe unless they have heard of him? And how can they hear unless there is someone to preach? (Romans 10:14 NAB).

Normally some other believer has to tell us the good news, whether individually, in an assembly, or through writing or another means of communication. Once we believe, we are received into the community of believers through Baptism:

For by one Spirit we were all baptized into one body (1 Corinthians 12:13).

We need other Christians to support us in our new-found faith, for we have turned away from the world and no longer have any support from the world:

"If you belonged to the world, it would love you as its own; the reason it hates you is that you do not belong to the world. But I chose you out of the world" (John 15:19 NAB).

Hopefully, we, in turn, will desire to bring God's word to others and support others in the community, whether through prayer, fellowship, or hands-on help:

> *All who believed were together and had all things in common; and they sold their possessions and goods and distributed them to all, as any had need. . . . And the Lord added to their number day by day those who were being saved* (*Acts* 2:44-46, 47).

> *The community of believers were of one heart and one mind. None of them ever claimed anything as his own; rather everything was held in common* (*Acts* 4:32 NAB).

It is just good common sense that two will succeed where one will fail:

> *Two are better than one, because they have a good reward for their toil. For if they fall, one will lift up his fellow; but woe to him who is alone when he falls and has not another to lift him up. Again, if two lie together, they are warm; but how can one be warm alone? And though a man might prevail against one who is alone, two will withstand him. A threefold cord is not quickly broken* (*Ecclesiastes* 4:9-12).

So we see that salvation takes place in a communal setting and that the community provides support. But is the community of the Church necessary for salvation? To answer this we must reflect on the very heart of God, the mystery of the Holy Trinity: "*God is love*" (*1 John* 4:8).

God's very nature is to love. The mutual love of the Father, Son, and Holy Spirit is complete in every way. Nor can God help loving us and all the creatures He has made. In addition, he has created us with the capacity to love as He loves. Our sins severely damage or even destroy our capacity to love. This is why God hates sin—because it is an obstacle to love, directly opposed to His very nature. Jesus restored our capacity to love by His sacrificial Passion and death on the cross, the ultimate expression of love.

In this is love, not that we loved God but that he loved us and sent his Son to be the expiation for our sins (1 John 4:10).

Our salvation depends on our response to this incredible love; on how we love God and neighbor in return:

And behold, a lawyer stood up to put him to the test, saying, "Teacher, what shall I do to inherit eternal life?" He said to him, "What is written in the law? How do you read?" And he answered, "You shall love the Lord your God with all your heart, and with all your soul, and with all your strength, and with all your mind; and your neighbor as yourself." And he said to him, "You have answered right; do this, and you will live" (Luke 10:25-28).

St. John clarifies this love of God further:

One who has no love for the brother he has seen cannot love the God he has not seen (1 John 4:20 NAB).

So the first point, then, is that our salvation depends on our love of God and our love of our brothers and sisters in the human family. This is because God is love and has made us like Himself.

The second point is that love tends toward union:

When he had finished speaking to Saul, the soul of Jonathan was knit to the soul of David, and Jonathan loved him as his own soul. . . . Then Jonathan made a covenant with David, because he loved him as his own soul (1 Samuel 18:1, 3).

"For this reason a man shall leave his father and mother and be joined to his wife, and the two shall become one flesh." This mystery is a profound one, and I am saying that it refers to Christ and the church (Ephesians 5:31-32).

We cannot draw close to God without drawing close to each other. If two or three people were to come to meet you at the center of a room, they would at the same time have come closer to each other. Similarly, when our loving Father draws His children to Himself, they are by that action drawn together with each other.

The argument, in brief, is as follows:

1) If we must love God and one another to be saved;

2) and if love always draws us together in union with the beloved;

   then it follows that we must be united with our Christian brothers and sisters in order to be saved. That is to say, "common unity" or "community" is necessary for salvation.

But the Body of Christ is much more than a support group. There is a deep oneness among Christians which springs from the unity of the Most Holy Trinity.

There are many kinds of unity. We have all experienced limited "oneness" with others, perhaps agreement in some particular interest. Two people can be united in their politics, or in their temperament, or in a project they are working on.

God is a "community" or "family" of three Persons, united so totally in love, in mind, heart, spirit, and in every other way as to be One God. Trinity means "Tri-unity" or "unity of the Three." Since we have been created in the image and likeness of God, we also have "community-ness" built into us.

Because of sin, we have become divided, isolated from one another and from God. This shattering of community is so great a tragedy that Jesus died to repair it. Only hours before His Passion, Jesus prayed:

> *"I do not pray for these only, but also for those who believe in me through their word, that they may all be one; even as thou Father, art in me, and I in thee, that they also may be in us, so that the world may believe that thou hast sent me" (John 17:20-21).*

Jesus hates division, anything that breaks the unity of love. St. Paul, in writing to the Corinthians, ranks discord or dissension within the Body of Christ among the worst of sins:

> *I beg you, brothers, in the name of our Lord, Jesus Christ, to agree in what you say. Let there be no factions; rather, be united in mind and judgment. I have been informed, my brothers, by certain members of Chloe's household that you are quarreling among yourselves* (*1 Corinthians* 1:10-11 NAB).

> *While there is jealousy and strife among you, are you not of the flesh, and behaving like ordinary men?* (*1 Corinthians* 3:3).

> *It is obvious what proceeds from the flesh: lewd conduct, impurity, licentiousness, idolatry, sorcery, **hostilities, bickering, jealousy, outbursts of rage, selfish rivalries, dissensions, factions, envy,** drunkenness, orgies, and the like. I warn you, as I have warned you before: those who do such things will not inherit the kingdom of God!* (*Galatians* 5:19-21 NAB, emphasis added).

Unity in the church, like the unity of the Holy Trinity, is brought about only by the Holy Spirit.

> *Make every effort to preserve the unity which has the Spirit as its origin and peace as its binding force. There is but one body and one Spirit* (*Ephesians* 4:3 NAB).

What is the unity of believers like? One of the best comparisons we can make is to the human body:

> *For just as the body is one and has many members, and all the members of the body, though many are one body, so it is with Christ* (*1 Corinthians* 12:12).

The members of the Body are equal in dignity, value, and worth:

> *Even those members of the body which seem less
> important are in fact indispensable. . . . God has so
> constructed the body as to give greater honor to the
> lowly members, that there may be no dissension in the
> body, but that all the members may be concerned for
> one another. If one member suffers, all the members
> suffer with it; if one member is honored, all the mem-
> bers share its joy. You, then, are the body of Christ.
> Every one of you is a member of it (1 Corinthians*
> 12:22, 24-27 NAB).*

The members differ, however, in their function or position in
the Body.

> *Just as each of us has one body with many members,
> and not all the members have the same function, so too
> we, though many, are one body in Christ and individu-
> ally members one of another (Romans* 12:4-5 NAB).

Different members may have very different gifts according to
their place in the Body:

> *And his gifts were that some should be apostles, some
> prophets, some evangelists, some pastors and teach-
> ers, to equip the saints for the work of ministry, for
> building up the body of Christ (Ephesians* 4:11-12).

> *Are all apostles? Are all prophets? Are all teachers?
> Do all work miracles or have the gift of healing? Do
> all speak in tongues, all have the gift of interpretation
> of tongues? (1 Corinthians* 12:29-30 NAB).

It is essential to the proper working of the Body that each
member accept its niche in the "ecology" of the Body. To
attempt to deny one's true identity and take another's part only
leads to trouble. Let's say God has created one member to be a
hand, and given it all the resources to be a good hand. What if
this member decides it wants to be an ear and could place itself
where the ear should be? We would call the result grotesque,
monstrous, unnatural. It would not be a good ear or a good
hand, and the whole body would suffer as a result. And so it is
in the Body of Christ.

Our attitude, to be in the spirit of community, in the spirit of love, must be oriented toward others and away from self:

> *I try to please all in any way I can by seeking, not my own advantage, but that of the many, that they may be saved (1 Corinthians 10:33 NAB).*
>
> *Since you have set your hearts on spiritual gifts, try to be rich in those that build up the church (1 Corinthians 14:12 NAB).*
>
> *Complete my joy by being of the same mind, having the same love, being in full accord and of one mind. Do nothing from selfishness or conceit, but in humility count others better than yourselves. Let each of you look not only to his own interests, but also to the interests of others (Philippians 2:2-4).*

* * *

The oneness of the Body of Christ is both invisible and visible. In Jesus Christ, everything, visible and invisible, material and spiritual, is brought into one:

> *God has given us the wisdom to understand fully the mystery, the plan he was pleased to decree in Christ, to be carried out in the fullness of time: namely, to bring all things in the heavens and on earth into one under Christ's headship (Ephesians 1:9-10 NAB).*

Just as Jesus the Head is both human and divine, so is His Body, the Church a marvelous composite of two realms (see *Colossians* 1:18). To say either that the Church is only invisible or only visible would be to miss this fundamental truth. Those who see only a human institution are blind to the underlying union of heart, mind, and spirit which is the foundation of the visible structure. Those who believe in a Church that exists only in the realm of the spirit forget that we are whole human beings with bodies as well as souls, and that we are meant to dwell for a while in the material world.

All those who are in union with Jesus are also in union with each other. This is why forgiveness is so important. If I am not in union with my brother, I cannot be in union with Christ. It also works the other way: if I am not in union with Jesus, I cannot have real union with my brother.

This union in Christ is a communion in love. It is a union of mind as well, a union of faith and belief. It is a union that encompasses all boundaries; even death is not a barrier to this "communion of the saints";

> *For I am sure that neither death . . . nor anything else*
> *in all creation, will be able to separate us from the love*
> *of God in Christ Jesus our Lord* (*Romans* 8:38, 39).

Catholics believe that this union of all the saints becomes deepest during the Mass when we receive Holy Communion, the Body and Blood of Christ. This is the moment when we are closest to Jesus and to those who are one with Him, whether our brother next to us, our sister on the other side of the earth, or our loved one who has died in Christ.

Every act of love benefits the whole Body; every sinful act wounds the whole Body. We can benefit others in the Body of Christ by beseeching God on their behalf; they in turn can intercede to God for us.

We can especially turn to Mary, the mother of Jesus and our mother:

> *Seeing his mother there with the disciple whom he*
> *loved, Jesus said to his mother, "Woman, there is your*
> *son." In turn he said to the disciple, "There is your*
> *mother." From that hour onward, the disciple took her*
> *into his care* (*John* 19:26-27 NAB).

Mary's words in the Bible are few, but they indicate her complete "yes" to God: *"And Mary said, 'Behold, I am the handmaid of the Lord; let it be to me according to your word'"* (*Luke* 1:38).

Her advice at the wedding feast of Cana is fitting for us today: *"His mother said to the servants, 'Do whatever he tells you'"* (*John* 2:5).

* * *

The teaching of Jesus is more than just His words. God used Jesus' whole life to speak to us; what He said, what He did, the love with which He did everything, His character, Who He is. He spent three years, night and day, with the Twelve He had chosen, time for them to get to know Him, time to ask questions, time to watch, time to wonder, time to pray. It would be up to them to pass on His teaching after He had ascended to the right hand of the Father. Despite all their time with Jesus, however, the apostles proved by their actions during His Passion and death that they were woefully under-prepared to take the Gospel to the whole world. It was not until they had received the Holy Spirit that they were fully equipped to step into Jesus' shoes. The Holy Spirit completed their knowledge of the deep things of God and also was always with them to refresh their memories:

> *"This much have I told you while I was still with you; the Paraclete, the Holy Spirit whom the Father will send in my name, will instruct you in everything, and remind you of all that I told you"* (*John* 14:25-26 NAB).

> *"I have yet many things to say to you, but you cannot bear them now. When the Spirit of truth comes, he will guide you into all the truth"* (*John* 16:12-13).

The Holy Spirit also empowered them to be effective witnesses to the Gospel of Jesus:

> *"You shall receive power when the Holy Spirit has come upon you: and you shall be my witnesses . . . to the end of the earth"* (*Acts* 1:8).

In the very early Church, before the Scriptures were written down, the preaching of the apostles was the only source of divine revelation. But after the death of the apostles, the Lord Jesus did not abandon the Church to drift without direction.

In the Catholic Church, we believe that the apostles appointed successors, who in turn appointed further successors, so that the apostolic witness to the risen Jesus has continued unbroken throughout the ages. We believe that the bishops are the present day successors to the apostles. We further believe that Peter held a special place among the apostles:

> *"The names of the twelve apostles are these:* **first,** *Simon, who is called Peter . . ." (Matthew* 10:2, emphasis added).

> *"Simon, Simon, behold, Satan demanded to have you, that he might sift you like wheat, but I have prayed for you that your faith may not fail; and when you have turned again, strengthen your brethren" (Luke* 22:31-32).

We believe Peter's office continues today in the person of the Bishop of Rome, the Pope. As Vicar (stand-in) of Christ on earth, we believe that he speaks with the authority of Jesus Himself, through the guidance of the Holy Spirit. Recall Jesus' words to Simon Peter:

> *"And I tell you, you are Peter, and on this rock I will build my church, and the powers of death shall not prevail against it. I will give you the keys of the kingdom of heaven, and whatever you bind on earth shall be bound in heaven, and whatever you loose on earth shall be loosed in heaven" (Matthew* 16:18-19).

In saying this, Jesus very likely had in mind the following verse from the prophet Isaiah:

> *And I will place on his shoulder the key of the house of David; he shall open, and none shall shut; and he shall shut, and none shall open (Isaiah* 22:22).

The context of this verse is the passing on of the dynasty of David from Shebna to Eliakim, suggesting that Jesus expected Peter one day to pass on the keys of the kingdom of Heaven to a successor. Even though it is Peter who wields the keys on earth, it is Jesus Christ Who at the same time *"'has the key of David, who opens and no one shall shut, who shuts and no one opens'" (Revelation* 3:7).

Some time after giving this authority to Peter, Jesus extended it to the other apostles:

> *"I assure you, whatever you declare bound on earth shall be held bound in heaven, and whatever you declare loosed on earth shall be held loosed in heaven" (Matthew* 18:18 NAB).

Jesus desires a very complete unity for us. He died on the cross that we might be of one heart, one mind, one Spirit, professing one faith, one hope, one love:

> *Now the company of those who believed were of one heart and soul (Acts* 4:32).

> *Complete my joy by being of the same mind, having the same love, being in full accord and of one mind (Philippians* 2:2).

> *Make every effort to preserve the unity which has the Spirit as its origin and peace as its binding force. There is but one body and one Spirit, just as there is but one hope given all of you by your call. There is one Lord, one faith, one baptism; one God and Father of all, who is over all, and works through all, and is in all (Ephesians* 4:3-6 NAB).

In the real world, it is not possible to have such a total unity without a visible unifying agent. The sheer number of denominations proves that the Sacred Scriptures, in themselves, are not a sufficient means for this unity. Each of these denominations was formed by someone dedicated to Jesus who was convinced that his interpretation of Scripture was the correct one. And yet there is only one faith, only one truth. Certainly Jesus would have provided the means for achieving the unity He so longed for!

Catholics believe that Peter, at the head of the apostles, and the popes in unbroken succession to this day at the head of the bishops, provide the required visible unifying agent. Catholics believe that the Pope, guided by the Holy Spirit, has supreme authority in the areas of teaching and governing the People of God.

Apostleship is passed on through the sacrament of Holy Orders. The outward sign of Holy Orders is the laying on of hands by the bishop. St. Paul refers to this in his letter of encouragement to Timothy: *"I remind you to stir into flame the gift of God bestowed on you when my hands were laid on you"* (*2 Timothy* 1:6 NAB).

There are three "degrees" to Holy Orders: bishops, who receive the fullness of the sacrament (see *1 Timothy* 3:1), presbyters or priests, who are the co-workers of the bishops (see *Titus* 1:5), and deacons, who are not ordained to priesthood but for tasks of service (see *Acts* 6:1-6).

All of the baptized share in the priesthood of Jesus Who is *"high priest after the order of Melchizedek"* (*Hebrews* 5:10). The ordained priesthood is at the service of the priesthood of all the baptized by building up the Church (see *Ephesians* 4:11-12). The ordained priesthood acts especially in the person of Christ the *Head,* unlike the priesthood of all the baptized.

Holy Orders and the Eucharist are specially interlinked. Catholics believe that only an ordained priest is able to bring the Real Presence of Jesus to the altar during Mass. Holy Thursday, therefore, the commemoration of the Last Supper, has special significance for the ordained priesthood. Just as Jesus fed the five thousand with ordinary bread through the Twelve, so He feeds us with the heavenly bread through the ordained priesthood. When we recall that the Eucharist is the "source and summit" of the Church's activity, the necessity of the ordained priesthood for salvation becomes apparent.

* * *

Perhaps, at this point, we are in a position to answer the questions brought up in the Introduction. Can both Catholics and other Christians be saved? Will our families, though divided on earth, be together in heaven?

To answer these questions, it is useful to ask, "How deeply divided are Christians on earth?" Is there not more that unites us than divides us? Are not all Christians included in the Body of Christ, which is the Church?

According to Catholic teaching, Jesus has only one Church, the one He founded on Peter (see *Matthew* 16:18).

> This Church . . . subsists in the Catholic Church. . . . Nevertheless, many elements of sanctification and truth are found outside its visible confines (Vatican II, *Lumen Gentium,* 8).

The word "subsist" was selected carefully by the Council Fathers. It stops short of saying that the Church of Jesus *is* the Catholic Church, but it is much stronger than saying that the Church of Jesus merely exists *within* the Catholic Church. Rather,

> the entirety of revealed truth, of sacraments, and of ministry that Christ gave for the building up of his Church and the carrying out of her mission is found within the Catholic communion of the Church (Pontifical Council for Promoting Christian Unity, *Directory for the Application of the Principles and Norms of Ecumenism,* 17).

This Church is necessary for salvation (see *Catechism of the Catholic Church* #846). But for those who

> do not have an opportunity to know or accept the gospel revelation or to enter the Church . . . salvation in Christ is accessible by virtue of a grace . . . [that] comes from Christ; it is the result of his Sacrifice and is communicated by the Holy Spirit (John Paul II, Encyclical Letter, *Redemptoris Missio,* 10).

Not all who profess faith in Jesus Christ belong fully to the Catholic Church:

> "Fully incorporated into the society of the Church are those who, possessing the Spirit of Christ, accept all

the means of salvation given to the Church together with her entire organization" (*Catechism of the Catholic Church* #837).

Christians—that is those who profess belief in Christ and are baptized—who do not fully belong to the Catholic Church are accepted by Catholics as brothers in the Lord (see *Catechism of the Catholic Church* #818). They are joined to the Church in many ways, even though their communion with the Catholic Church is imperfect (see *Catechism of the Catholic Church* #838).

> "Many elements of sanctification and of truth" are found outside the visible confines of the Catholic Church: "the written Word of God; the life of grace; faith, hope, and charity, with the other interior gifts of the Holy Spirit, as well as visible elements" (*Catechism of the Catholic Church* #819).

Who, then, can be saved according to Catholic teaching?

> "Those who, through no fault of their own, do not know the Gospel of Christ or his Church, but who nevertheless seek God with a sincere heart, and, moved by grace, try in their actions to do his will as they know it through the dictates of their conscience—those too may achieve eternal salvation" (*Catechism of the Catholic Church* #847).

> "They could not be saved who, knowing that the Catholic Church was founded as necessary by God through Christ, would refuse either to enter it or to remain in it" (*Catechism of the Catholic Church* #846).

The key word here is "knowing." If a person "knows as true" that he should enter or remain in the Catholic Church in order to be saved, and refuses to do so, this would amount to acting against one's conscience.

*But if a man eats when his conscience has misgivings
about eating, he is already condemned, because he is
not acting in accordance with what he believes.
Whatever does not accord with one's belief is sinful
(Romans 14:23 NAB).*

Just being a member of the Catholic Church, of course, is of
itself no guarantee of salvation:

"Even though incorporated into the Church, one who
does not however persevere in charity is not saved. He
remains indeed in the bosom of the Church, but 'in
body' not 'in heart'" (*Catechism of the Catholic
Church* #837).

Section 5

ROADBLOCKS TO SALVATION

The major section of this book has addressed the question, "What must I do to be saved?" Now we look at the opposite question, "What must I avoid to be saved?"

There are definite behaviors that, unrepented, will keep a person out of the Kingdom of God:

> *And God spoke all these words, saying,*
>
> *"I, the LORD, am your God, who brought you out of the land of Egypt, that place of slavery. You shall not have other gods besides me. . . .*
>
> *"You shall not take the name of the LORD, your God, in vain. . . .*
>
> *"Remember to keep holy the sabbath day. . . .*
>
> *"Honor your father and your mother. . . .*
>
> *"You shall not kill.*
>
> *"You shall not commit adultery.*
>
> *"You shall not steal.*
>
> *"You shall not bear false witness against your neighbor.*
>
> *"You shall not covet your neighbor's house. You shall not covet your neighbor's wife . . . nor anything else that belongs to him"* (*Exodus* 20:1-3, 7, 8, 12, 13-17 NAB).

Can you not realize that the unholy will not fall heir to the kingdom of God? Do not deceive yourselves: no fornicators, idolaters, or adulterers, no sexual perverts, thieves, misers, or drunkards, no slanderers or robbers will inherit God's kingdom (1 Corinthians 6:9-10 NAB).

It is obvious what proceeds from the flesh: lewd conduct, impurity, licentiousness, idolatry, sorcery, hostilities, bickering, jealousy, outbursts of rage, selfish rivalries, dissensions, factions, envy, drunkenness, orgies, and the like. I warn you, as I have warned you before: those who do such things will not inherit the kingdom of God! (Galatians 5:19-21 NAB).

For those who are factious and do not obey the truth, but obey wickedness, there will be wrath and fury (Romans 2:8).

There are six things which the LORD hates, yes, seven are an abomination to him; haughty eyes, a lying tongue, and hands that shed innocent blood; a heart that plots wicked schemes, feet that run swiftly to evil, the false witness who utters lies, and he who sows discord among brothers (Proverbs 6:16-19 NAB).

Jesus speaks in the strongest language against those who lead the innocent astray:

"Whoever causes one of these little ones who believe in me to sin, it would be better for him if a great millstone were hung round his neck and he were thrown into the sea. And if your hand causes you to sin, cut it off; it is better for you to enter life maimed than with two hands go to hell, to the unquenchable fire" (Mark 9:42-43).

Sins against God Himself are the worst:

Whoever sacrifices to any god, save the LORD only, shall be utterly destroyed (Exodus 22:20).

You cannot drink the cup of the Lord and also the cup

of demons. You cannot partake of the table of the Lord and likewise the table of demons (1 Corinthians 10:21 NAB).

Jesus hates hypocrisy—sin-blindness which prevents people from coming to Him for salvation, healing, and restoration:

"Woe to you, scribes and Pharisees, hypocrites! for you cleanse the outside of the cup and of the plate, but inside they are full of extortion and rapacity. You blind Pharisee! first cleanse the inside of the cup and of the plate, that the outside also may be clean" (Matthew 23:25-26).

Woe to those who call evil good, and good evil, who change darkness into light, and light into darkness, who change bitter into sweet and sweet into bitter! (Isaiah 5:20 NAB).

Speaking of the scribes and Pharisees on another occasion, Jesus said, " 'They are blind guides. And if a blind man leads a blind man, both will fall into a pit' " (*Matthew* 15:14). Sin is the major cause of spiritual blindness. To refuse to worship the true God is to invite disaster:

For the wrath of God is revealed from heaven against all ungodliness and wickedness of men who by their wickedness suppress the truth. For what can be known about God is plain to them, because God has shown it to them. . . . Although they knew God they did not honor him as God or give thanks to him, but they became futile in their thinking and their senseless minds were darkened. Claiming to be wise, they became fools (Romans 1:18-19, 21-22).

If we are only going through the motions in our worship, our spiritual vision will dim. Inspiration from the LORD will vanish:

Stupefy yourselves and be in a stupor, blind yourselves and be blind! Be drunk, but not with wine; stagger, but not with strong drink! For the LORD has poured out

*upon you a spirit of deep sleep, and has closed your
eyes, the prophets, and covered your heads, the
seers. . . . "Because this people draw near me with
their mouth and honor me with their lips, while their
hearts are far from me" (Isaiah 29:9-10, 13).*

When we fail to worship the only true God, it is because we
have become hypnotized by a false god. What is apparent to the
little children (see *Luke* 10:21), is hidden from those who do not
believe:

*If our gospel can be called "veiled" in any sense, it is
such only for those who are headed toward destruc-
tion. Their unbelieving minds have been blinded by
the god of the present age so that they do not see the
splendor of the gospel showing forth the glory of
Christ, the image of God (2 Corinthians 4:3-4 NAB).*

Even among those who appear to be living Godly lives, the possibility of self-deception exists. In fact, we cannot know our own
hearts:

*More tortuous than all else is the human heart, beyond
remedy; who can understand it? I, the LORD, alone
probe the mind and test the heart, to reward everyone
according to his ways, according to the merit of his
deeds (Jeremiah 17:9-10 NAB).*

St. Paul, whom we would certainly judge to be a holy man,
does not claim so for himself. He tells us:

*I do not even pass judgment on myself. Mind you, I
have nothing on my conscience. But that does not
mean that I am declaring myself innocent. The Lord is
the one to judge me, so stop passing judgment before
the time of his return. He will bring to light what is
hidden in darkness and manifest the intentions of
hearts. At that time, everyone will receive his praise
from God (1 Corinthians 4:3-5 NAB).*

St. Paul also encourages us to have a healthy concern for our spiritual well-being and warns us against complacency: *"Let anyone who thinks he is standing upright watch out lest he fall!"* (*1 Corinthians* 10:12 NAB).

We have an enemy whose most effective weapon against us is deception. This, combined with our inclination to wander from the truth, is enough reason to live a lifestyle of continual turning back to the Lord:

> *The coming of the lawless one by the activity of Satan will be with all power and with pretended signs and wonders, and with all wicked deception for those who are to perish, because they refused to love the truth and so be saved* (*2 Thessalonians* 2:9-10).

Conclusion

We have allowed the Scriptures to speak. Hopefully an overall picture has emerged to answer the question "What must I do to be saved." By way of summary, we have chosen a few Scriptures which capture the essence of the Christian life, the joyful road to heaven:

> *Because you are God's chosen ones, holy and beloved, clothe yourselves with heartfelt mercy, with kindness, humility, meekness, and patience. Bear with one another; forgive whatever grievances you have against one another. Forgive as the Lord has forgiven you. Over all these virtues put on love, which binds the rest together and makes them perfect. Christ's peace must reign in your hearts, since as members of the one body you have been called to that peace. Dedicate yourselves to thankfulness. Let the word of Christ, rich as it is, dwell in you. In wisdom made perfect, instruct and admonish one another. Sing gratefully to God from your hearts in psalms, hymns, and inspired songs. Whatever you do, whether in speech or in action, do it in the name of the Lord Jesus. Give thanks to God the Father through him (Colossians 3:12-17 NAB).*

St. Peter teaches us to build a ladder which goes, step by step, from faith to love. This group of characteristics, built up over time, describes the path of Christian growth from beginning to end:

> *For this reason make every effort to supplement your faith with virtue, and virtue with knowledge, and*

111

knowledge with self-control, and self-control with steadfastness, and steadfastness with godliness, and godliness with brotherly affection, and brotherly affection with love (2 Peter 1:5-7).

Jesus said, *" 'You will know them by their fruits' "* (*Matthew* 7:16), and *"the fruit of the Spirit is love, joy, peace, patient endurance, kindness, generosity, faith, mildness, and chastity"* (*Galatians* 5:22-23 NAB). When others observe the fruit of the Holy Spirit coming forth and ripening in our lives, we will know the kingdom of God has seized new ground from the kingdom of the world.

St. Paul lists a grab bag of do's and don'ts for the Christian:

Let love be genuine; hate what is evil, hold fast to what is good; love one another with brotherly affection; outdo one another in showing honor. Never flag in zeal, be aglow with the Spirit, serve the Lord. Rejoice in your hope, be patient in tribulation, be constant in prayer. Contribute to the needs of the saints, practice hospitality. Bless those who persecute you; bless and do not curse them. Rejoice with those who rejoice, weep with those who weep. Live in harmony with one another; do not be haughty, but associate with the lowly; never be conceited. Repay no one evil for evil, but take thought for what is noble in the sight of all. If possible, so far as it depends upon you, live peaceably with all (Romans 12:9-18).

The Gospel of Jesus Christ is not hard to understand; it has the simplicity of truth. The bottom line: it all comes down to our hearts. We must believe, really, and love, really. If we do, the love of Christ flows out of us unstoppably. *" 'For out of the abundance of the heart the mouth speaks' "* (*Matthew* 12:34). *" 'Out of [your] heart shall flow rivers of living water' "* (*John* 7:38). The barren desert around us becomes transformed into a life-giving oasis. *"He turns a desert into pools of water, a parched land into springs of water"* (*Psalm* 107:35).

When we love as Jesus loves:

> *then will the eyes of the blind be opened, the ears of the deaf be cleared; then will the lame leap like a stag, then the tongue of the dumb will sing. Streams will burst forth in the desert and rivers in the steppe. The burning sands will become pools, and the thirsty ground, springs of water. . . . Those whom the LORD has ransomed will return and enter Zion singing, crowned with everlasting joy; they will meet with joy and gladness, sorrow and mourning will flee (Isaiah 35:5-7, 10 NAB).*

Suggested Reading

Barclay, William. *The Daily Bible Series: Revised edition.* The Westminster Press, Philadelphia, 1975.

Catechism of the Catholic Church. English Translation, 1994. See especially Nos. 1987-2029.

Keating, Karl. *What Catholics Really Believe—Setting the Record Straight: 52 Answers to Common Misconceptions about the Catholic Faith.* Servant Publications, Ann Arbor, 1992.

Pillar of Fire, Pillar of Truth. Catholic Answers, San Diego, 1993.

Schreck, Alan. *Catholic and Christian: An Explanation of Commonly Misunderstood Catholic Beliefs.* Servant Books, Ann Arbor, 1984.

Sheed, F. J. *Theology for Beginners.* Third Edition, Servant Books, Ann Arbor, 1981.

Stravinskas, Peter M. J. *The Catholic Response.* Our Sunday Visitor, Inc., Huntington, Ind., 1985.

Vatican Council II: The Conciliar and Post Conciliar Documents. New Revised Edition. Austin Flannery, O.P., ed. Liturgical Press, Collegeville, MN 56321, 1975 and 1984.

Vatican Council II: More Post Conciliar Documents. Austin Flannery, O.P., ed. Liturgical Press, Collegeville, MN 56321, 1982.

SCRIPTURAL INDEX

116